"Part of an emergent wave of urgently needed new media research, *Crime, Justice and Social Media* promises to serve as a foundational primer on the relationship between online media environments and technosocial criminality. In his unwavering analysis of how gender inequalities and asymmetries structure online harms and transgressions, Michael Salter illuminates the powerful contradictions, tensions, and amplifications of harm in social media, while remaining faithful to the complex emancipatory potential of new modes of feminist online contestation, resistance, and justice-seeking pursuits."

Michelle Brown, Associate Professor, Department of Sociology, University of Tennessee, USA, and co-editor of Crime, Media, Culture

"This book uses case studies of online abuse and focus group data taken from research with young people in Australia to develop a set of cogent arguments that propose such abuse intersects with established patterns of inequality, but also to show how social media has emancipatory potential, and is challenging conventional ways of understanding crime and injustice. Advocating for a critical theory of online abuse using contemporary empirical examples, the book offers particularly useful insights for scholars and students interested in the role of social media in the commission of crimes as well as in justice-seeking initiatives."

Greg Martin, Associate Professor of Socio-Legal Studies, University of Sydney, Australia

"Online abuse involves new media affordances alongside systemic patterns of discrimination. By examining coordinated harassment campaigns in relation to a broader media culture, Dr. Salter provides a nuanced and convincing account of weaponised visibility. This timely book is recommended for students, researchers and practitioners who are coming to terms with these issues."

Daniel Trottier, Assistant Professor, Department of Media and Communication, Erasmus University Rotterdam, the Netherlands

"This lively, thought provoking book greatly enlarges our understanding of online abuse across various social media platforms. Its lucid combination of critical theory, analytical insight, and interdisciplinary sensibility make it indispensable reading for anyone seeking to know more about this vital aspect of contemporary culture. In particular, its attention to the gendered dynamics and politics of abuse make it a timely, bold and innovative statement of criminology at its very best."

Eamonn Carrabine, Professor of Sociology, University of Essex, UK, and co-editor of Crime, Media, Culture

CRIME, JUSTICE AND SOCIAL MEDIA

How is social media changing contemporary understandings of crime and injustice, and what contribution can it make to justice-seeking? Abuse on social media often involves betrayals of trust and invasions of privacy that range from the public circulation of intimate photographs to mass campaigns of public abuse and harassment using platforms such as Facebook, Twitter, 8chan and Reddit – forms of abuse that disproportionately target women and children.

Crime, Justice and Social Media argues that online abuse is not discontinuous with established patterns of inequality but rather intersects with and amplifies them. Embedded within social media platforms are inducements to abuse and harass other users who are rarely provided with the tools to protect themselves or interrupt the abuse of others. There is a relationship between the values that shape the technological design and administration of social media, and those that inform the use of abuse and harassment to exclude and marginalise diverse participants in public life.

Drawing on original qualitative research, this book is essential reading for students and scholars in the fields of cyber-crime, media and crime, cultural criminology, and gender and crime.

Michael Salter is a Senior Lecturer in Criminology in the School of Social Sciences and Psychology at Western Sydney University, Australia.

NEW DIRECTIONS IN CRITICAL CRIMINOLOGY

Edited by Walter S. DeKeseredy, West Virginia University, USA

This series presents new cutting-edge critical criminological empirical, theoretical, and policy work on a broad range of social problems, including drug policy, rural crime and social control, policing and the media, ecocide, intersectionality and the gendered nature of crime. It aims to highlight the most up-to-date authoritative essays written by new and established scholars in the field. Rather than offering a survey of the literature, each book takes a strong position on topics of major concern to those interested in seeking new ways of thinking critically about crime.

For a full list of titles in this series, please visit www.routledge.com.

CRIME, JUSTICE AND SOCIAL MEDIA

Michael Salter

Routledge
Taylor & Francis Group

LONDON AND NEW YORK

First published 2017
by Routledge
2 Park Square, Milton Park, Abingdon, Oxon OX14 4RN

and by Routledge
711 Third Avenue, New York, NY 10017

Routledge is an imprint of the Taylor & Francis Group, an informa business

British Library Cataloguing in Publication Data
A catalogue record for this book is available from the British Library

Library of Congress Cataloging in Publication Data
Names: Salter, Michael, 1980– author.
Title: Crime, justice and social media / Michael Salter.
Description: Abingdon, Oxon ; New York, NY : Routledge, 2016. | Series: New directions in critical criminology ; 14 | Includes bibliographical references and index.
Identifiers: LCCN 2016007981| ISBN 9781138919662 (hardback) | ISBN 9781138919679 (pbk.) | ISBN 9781315687742 (ebook)
Subjects: LCSH: Social media. | Computer crimes–Social aspects. | Online sexual predators. | Cyberbullying. | Internet–Moral and ethical aspects. | Privacy, Right of. | Exploitation. | Criminal justice, Administration of.
Classification: LCC HM742 .S254 2016 | DDC 302.23/1–dc23
LC record available at https://lccn.loc.gov/2016007981

ISBN: 978-1-138-91966-2 (hbk)
ISBN: 978-1-138-91967-9 (pbk)
ISBN: 978-1-315-68774-2 (ebk)

Typeset in Bembo
by Taylor & Francis Books

CONTENTS

ACKNOWLEDGEMENT

Thanks to everyone who has provided much-needed encouragement from the inception of this book to its completion. I appreciate the ongoing support of the School of Social Sciences and Psychology at Western Sydney University, which provided me with a six-month sabbatical that enabled me to focus on completing the manuscript. My editor Tom Sutton at Routledge has been a terrific help and I've benefitted from Hannah Catterall's editorial assistance. Thank you to Professor Rob Stones and Dr Amy Shields Dobson for their useful feedback and comments on chapters. I'd also like to thank the Crime and Justice Research Centre at Queensland University of Technology, where I wrote and presented Chapter 6 while a Visiting Fellow in September 2015. The focus group research upon which Chapters 3, 4 and 5 are based was funded by the Australian Institute of Criminology. I'm particularly indebted to Paul Brace who has read and commented on drafts and put up with me throughout the writing process. Finally, thanks to Mum and Dad for everything.

INTRODUCTION

In June 2015, it was widely reported in Australia that a significant number of nude and intimate images of Australian women had been uploaded to the image-board site 8chan without the consent of the women depicted (news.com.au, 2015). 8chan is one of a number of so-called 'chan' image-board sites that have attracted attention as platforms for anonymous online transgression, ranging from minor pranks to significant breaches of privacy. When women contacted the 8chan administrator, American software developer Fredrick Brennan, to request the removal of their images, his response reflected the misogynist libertarianism for which the 'chan' boards have become infamous. After refusing to remove the photos without a formal legal order, Brennan disputed that the non-consensual circulation of the images on his site constituted genuine victimisation, since the humiliation of the women was simply 'the cost of being a slut'. He went on to write sarcastically that 'a woman who smiled with her tits uncovered is at one time strong and empowered and another time a victim, of course'.[1] The clear implication was that a woman who posed consensually for a nude photo could not legitimately claim victimhood if that photo was later circulated without her permission.

Links to the nude images spread widely through Facebook and other social media platforms. Victims reported multiple harassing contacts from men who had viewed the images and uncovered their identities.[2] Posters on 8chan are anonymous so, while a number of victims suggested that their malicious ex-partners were responsible, the individuals who originally uploaded the images without their consent could not be definitively identified. Mass media coverage of the incident was generally condemnatory of the people and site who circulated the images; however, popular morning television show Sunrise posted an article to its Facebook site asking 'What's it going to take for women to get the message about taking and sending nude photos'? Although articulated in more civil tones, this sentiment shared common ground with Brennan's position that public humiliation is the probable 'cost' of making intimate images, and hence victimised women share some responsibility for their plight. Underpinning this logic is the view that there is something inherently risky if not amoral about women making nude images of themselves, particularly when these are shared with other people.

Prominent Australian feminist and journalist Clementine Ford responded succinctly with a Facebook post of a photo of herself with 'Hey #Sunrise get fucked' written across her exposed chest (Ford, 2015). In the accompanying text, Ford expressed her exasperation at the victim-blaming logic of the Sunrise post:

> When will women learn? Learn what? That our bodies do not belong to us? That we have no right to determine who sees those bodies, touches those bodies, fucks those bodies, and shares in those bodies? Honey, we don't need to learn that. We already know the answer. We don't have those rights. We are not allowed to be the masters of ourselves, only the gatekeepers.
>
> *(original post deleted by Facebook, text available at Ford, 2015)*

In the face of pervasive victim-blaming, Ford's protest generated a counter-discourse that rejected the stigmatisation of women who make intimate images of themselves. At the time of writing, her post has been 'liked' over 300,000 times and 'shared' over 70,000 times. The television station publicly apologised for the 'insensitive' wording of their post and had it removed (news.com.au, 2015). The social media reception to Ford's protest included many expressions of support, such as women who also posted photos of themselves to social media with 'Hey

#Sunrise get fucked' written on their bodies. These women were both expressing solidarity with the victims of the 8chan leak and emphasising the rights of women to an intimate life free from invasions of privacy.

Ford's Facebook post attracted a mass of critical social media comments (mostly although not exclusively from male users) arguing that women are at least partially responsible when their intimate images are published online. Comments included:

> Here's a thought, why don't you stop taking nude photos or stop winging?

> So wait, you took pictures for others to see, yet complain when they are seen? Maybe instead attacking men, you should accept responsibility for your own actions? If you didnt take the pics, you wouldnt be in this situation now would you?

> If you are too dense to understand that sharing anything on the internet is at your risk that is not the problem of the rest of the world.

These arguments generally ignored the breach of privacy involved in the non-consensual circulation of the images on 8chan. Taking a nude photo and sharing it with an intimate partner was conflated with sharing the image with the internet. Responsibility for the circulation of the images on 8chan was thus devolved to the women depicted, not to those who circulated the images in the first place. This argument segued into slurs against women who make and send images of themselves as 'stupid' and 'retarded', and insults against Ford herself, who was attacked as a 'whore' and 'attention seeker'. Ford estimated that she received over 1,000 insults and threats in the two days following her post (Caggiano, 2015). These included both 'public' comments on her Facebook 'wall', but also 'private' messages via Facebook's Messenger function, in which some men attempted to solicit nude images from Ford, and others denigrated her appearance and sexuality (Ford, 2015).

Amongst these was 20-year-old Ryan Hawkins, who sent Ford two messages stating 'I'm going to rape and bash you stupid little slut' and calling her 'lesbian scum'. Ford screenshotted the threats and posted them to her public Facebook wall as an example of the kinds of online harassment she was receiving. Very quickly, Hawkins became the subject of considerable criticism on social media that was subsequently covered on newspapers and television. In a statement to the media, Hawkins said 'I was being a smart arse, just trying to have some sick fun with her, but it didn't really work' (Wright, 2015). He said he 'thought it was pretty obvious it was an empty threat, but I guess she didn't' and that Ford should have contacted him privately rather than publicly sharing the message. Initially, Ford intended to report Hawkins to the police (Wright, 2015) but decided not to make a formal complaint.

Abuse and harassment are in violation of Facebook's terms of service but it's unknown what if any action was taken by Facebook against Hawkins, or the hundreds of other users who used the service to abuse and threaten Ford. Ford, however, found herself banned from the service for 30 days, after Facebook determined that she had 'violated community standards' by screenshotting and posting Hawkins's threat to her Facebook wall (Wright, 2015). The ban was only lifted after Ford was able to contact and negotiate directly with Facebook representatives. She then posted this in response on June 21:

> No one should be punished for speaking out against abuse, especially not the kind of cowardly abuse sent under the banner of 'private correspondence'. Private correspondence is a conversation mutually entered into by more than one party and defined by respect and sometimes discretion. It is not someone sending you unsolicited emails calling you a filthy whore and sending you unasked for pictures of their dick. To argue otherwise is the same as suggesting that flashers or tram masturbators are owed some kind of respect and privacy. No. You do not have the right to have your violent hate speech kept secret from the world because you either lacked the courage to own it publicly or because you not so secretly get off on humiliating and degrading women in a way that relies on their isolation.[3]

Hawkins had insisted that his threats were personal and even semi-humorous ('sick fun') correspondence undeserving of a public response of the kind that Ford mounted. In the excerpt above, Ford forcefully resists the 'privatisation' of online abuse in light of Facebook's actions against her, which appeared to reinforce the notion that Hawkin's threat was a personal matter. She argued that to characterise online abuse as personal or private is to de-politicise and individualise it, maintaining victims of online abuse in a state of 'isolation' that increases the risk of abuse. Her position is that online abuse is a public issue, regardless of the online mode through which it is delivered, because it has significant effects on women both individually and as a group. If social media platforms or other authorities will not police this abuse, and their complaints mechanisms can indirectly reinforce the abuse, then she and others feel justified in enforcing accountability through other means. However, this in turn raises unresolved moral dilemmas. As technology journalist and commentator Asher Wolf (2015) observes:

> Vigilante action, pitchforks and fire aren't really the road to a happy society.
> And that's where we're going, isn't it? Naming, shaming, ganging up on horrible, awful perps, emailing their mothers, publicly and permanently burning down their reputations, jobs, and social connections... because that's the only option women feel they've been left with.

The complexity of this incident captures many of the themes of this book. Social media is not just a place where crime and justice are discussed; it's a place where crime happens, and so does justice-seeking. Online abuse on social media often involves betrayals of trust and invasions of privacy of the kind evident in the circulation of the women's images on 8chan. As this book shows, the non-consensual publication of intimate images is a form of humiliation that differentially impacts on women and girls. The initial response from Sunrise illustrates the continuity between online misogyny and prevailing sentiments within the mass media, where it is often inferred or stated outright that girls and women who experience online abuse are responsible for their plight. This book argues that online abuse is not discontinuous with established patterns of inequality but rather intersects with and can amplify them, often in unexpected forms.

At the same time, social media presents users with new discursive opportunities in which meaning-making about crime and justice can unfold in efficacious ways. In the incident above, Ford could use Facebook to launch a successful protest against victim-blaming on social media and the mass media. She circulated a feminist re-interpretation of erotic image-making as normal and pleasurable, and publicly exposed a man who threatened to physically and sexually assault her. The fact that Facebook viewed her public exposure of Hawkins's threats as a reason to ban her from the service is evidence of the highly ambiguous and contradictory response to online abuse that prevails across many platforms. Social media is host to debate and conflict over what constitutes crime and justice, and this conflict is evident not only between users but also between users and social media companies. A central argument of this book is that the prevalence of abuse on social media reflects a fundamental congruency between the values that shape the technological design and administration of social media, and those that inform the use of abuse and harassment to exclude and marginalise diverse participants in public life.

This book situates crime and justice on social media within a critical theory perspective, recognising that online abuse and justice-seeking takes shape within the communicative potentialities offered by social media. After providing a short history of the role of online abuse in shaping the development of social media, the first chapter provides a general overview of theoretical approaches to the issue before advocating for a critical theory of online abuse. The second chapter is a detailed examination of Gamergate, in which an act of online aggression by a male video game developer against his ex-partner in 2014 escalated into a mass movement of online abuse of unprecedented proportions. The chapter argues that the key role of social media in this collective project of online misogyny, and the sparse protections afforded to their targets by either social media companies or the police, demonstrates the instantiation of specific values and prerogatives within technological design reflective of broader social norms. The third chapter expands on this theme. This chapter draws on focus group research with young Australians aged 18–20 to describe how the underlying profit-driven architecture of social media encourages an instrumental attitude to oneself and others that makes online abuse more likely.[4] Importantly, this chapter shows that online abuse 'works' as a strategy for the accumulation of recognition, social capital and potentially income.

Chapter 4 examines how dominant gendered norms create the conditions in which online abuse is more likely to occur. The chapter focuses on how young people's production and circulation of images on social media is shaped by implicit and explicit asymmetries of power.

Against this backdrop, Chapter 5 discusses how online abuse takes shape within the gendered inequalities of young people's intimate and peer relationships. It focuses on the role of online abuse in the projection of particular forms of male power, as well as the opportunities that girls and women find to disrupt or decentre the double standards that regulate gender relations on social media. Taken together, these first five chapters examine online abuse as it manifests in intimate life, in peer relations and on a larger scale as rolling collective projects of harm. Chapter 6 uses two interlinked operations from the online collective Anonymous to ask important questions about the critical and emancipatory potentials of social media. How is social media changing contemporary under-standings of crime and injustice, and what contribution can it make to justice-seeking?

Key terms and social media platforms

On social media, the definition of what constitutes 'abuse' and 'harassment' is openly and ferociously contested. The line of delinea-tion between robust disagreement and outright abuse on social media (and elsewhere) can become blurry. It is therefore important to be clear about the foundational terms of this book. This book defines 'online abuse' as the misuse of social media and other online com-munication platforms with the intent to cause harm or offence to another person or persons. The term 'abuse' is sometimes used in the mass media and criminological literature as synonymous with 'sexual abuse' but that is not my intention here. Instead, the term 'abuse' refers to the misuse or misappropriation of the publicity offered by social media, typically involving the deliberate invasion of another person's privacy or the humiliating publication of (true or false) information about personal lives and characteristics. Less common although very serious forms of online criminality such as the use of social media by 'terror' groups or child sex offenders are not discussed in this book in any detail. These activities fall outside the book's general definition of 'online abuse' since the intentions of offenders are more complex than to 'cause harm or offence'. Chapter 6 takes a more expansive look at the transnationalising dimensions of social media but otherwise the book primarily addresses online abuse in the lives of young people and adults in Australia and the Global North more generally.

The book defines social media according to boyd and Ellison's (2007: 211) criteria: 'web-based services that allow individuals to (1) construct a public or semi-public profile within a bounded system, (2) articulate a list of other users with whom they share a connection, and (3) view and traverse their list of connections and those made by others within the system'. Van Dijk (2013: 8) suggests that social media sites have evolved four key categories, namely, 'social networking sites' such as Facebook that promote interpersonal contact, 'user-generated content' sites such as YouTube or Wikipedia that promote cultural collaboration and exchange, 'trading and marketing sites' that aim at exchanging or selling items, and finally 'play and game sites' that enable users to play online games. This book will be focused on social networking sites (particularly Facebook and Twitter) and user-generated content sites such as YouTube that have been most prominent in debates over online abuse and safety. While this book keeps social media as its main focus, it nonetheless recognises how communication flows into and from social media via other methods (such as email or smartphone messaging) and addresses how diverse technological affordances can impact on the progression of online abuse and responses to it.

A brief description of the main social media sites addressed in this book is provided below.

Facebook is currently the largest and most high-profile social media platform in the world. Since its launch in 2004, it has evolved from a website for Harvard College students to a global internet behemoth, reporting 1.49 billion monthly active users in 2015.[5] To use the site, individuals create a user profile based on their personal information and a picture of themselves, and then add other users as 'friends' with whom they can exchange content and messages. Facebook has positioned itself as the 'family friendly' and child-safe social media platform. The site seeks to ensure that users are registered under their legal name, and content uploaded to Facebook is actively monitored and censored by content moderators to ensure its compliance with Facebook's terms of service.

Twitter is an influential 'micro-blogging' social media site. Launched in 2006, it recorded 310 million monthly active users in 2015.[6] Like

Facebook, Twitter users create a profile about themselves using image and text. Unlike Facebook, Twitter user profiles can be pseudonymous and contain no identifying information about the user. Users then 'follow' one another, and read or post 'tweets' which are short 140-character messages. Twitter is known for hosting more politically orientated discourse and has proven popular with journalists, politicians and other public figures. As the resources of 'old media' shrink (in part due to the impact of social media), Twitter has come to play a notable role in shaping the daily news agenda.

YouTube is a video-sharing website that allows users to upload, view and share videos. It was purchased in 2006 by Google after its launch in 2005, and reportedly over a billion different users visit the site each month (Reuters 2013). YouTube pioneered the online streaming (rather than downloading) of video, which has made it palatable to a wide range of commercial content providers looking for a viable solution to the scourge of internet piracy. Although user-generated content was dominant during the initial phase of YouTube, professionally generated content such as music videos and television programmes now drives a significant proportion of views. Nonetheless, YouTube provides a platform in which video bloggers (or 'vloggers') can amass followers and generate income through YouTube's advertising strategies, as well as product placement or endorsements.

Snapchat is a mobile-device only application (unlike Facebook, Twitter and YouTube, which can be accessed on a computer or mobile device such as a phone or tablet) that allows users to exchange photos, video and text. The major point of difference with other social media platforms is that Snapchat content can only be viewed for up to 10 seconds, at which point it is automatically deleted. Snapchat owes much of its popularity to public concern about young people 'sexting' or exchanging nude photos of one another. The service offers users some assurance that 'private' images such as nude pictures cannot be recirculated without their consent.[7] Although its salacious reputation undoubtedly drives user interest, it appears that most users don't use the service to send nude or sexual material, but instead send spontaneous, comedic and self-parodying material such as making 'stupid faces' (Roesner et al., 2014). Snapchat is estimated to have over 200 million monthly users (Morrison, 2015).

Although relatively 'low tech' in contrast to the sleek interfaces of social media, bulletin boards and image-boards play a central role in the generation and dissemination of online content and discourse. An overview of Reddit, 4chan and 8chan is below.

Reddit operates essentially as a bulletin board system, in which registered members can create their own discussion boards ('subreddits') on any topic they wish, and users ('redditors') then post text and website links in an unfolding conversation with one another. Redditors rank each other's content by 'up' or 'down' voting it, pushing popular submissions to the top of the discussion. Reddit is a very popular site with over 200 million unique visitors each month.[8] While it hosts subreddits on virtually every imaginable topic (and many unimaginable ones), Reddit is notorious for its libertarian 'free speech' ethos and policy of non-intervention, in which redditors have been free to establish and run misogynist, racist and homophobic subreddits hosting offensive and quasi-legal material.

4chan is an image-board website launched in 2003. It continued to attract over 22 million monthly users in 2012 (Chen, 2012). It has significant cultural influence as the origin of many well-known internet 'memes' (semi-obscure jokes). As an image-board, it operates primarily through the posting of images that can then be commented upon, usually by anonymous participants. Its 'random' board (often just called /b/, since its URL is http://boards.4chan.org/b/) has become notorious for orchestrated pranks and campaigns of abuse. The 'politically incorrect' or /pol/ board is well known for its white supremacist and misogynist ethos. Other members of 4chan have turned their penchant for provocation into public activism with the emergence of Anonymous, a loose collective of online activists (Coleman, 2014). As Chapter 6 discusses, a 'hacktivist' permutation of Anonymous now operates largely independently from 4chan, although the term Anonymous (or the singular 'anon') may still be applied to 4chan and its participants.

8chan was launched in 2013 by software developer Frank Brennan, after he decided that administrators exerted too much control over 4chan. Cleaving more closely to a radical free-speech, anti-censorship ethos, 8chan has become notorious for hosting extreme content and providing links to child abuse material. It saw a significant boost in traffic in September 2014 when 4chan banned discussion of Gamergate (to be discussed in Chapter 2). It's /baphomet/ board has become known for the orchestration of harassing and potentially dangerous pranks that have included 'swatting', or sending false tips to the police to trigger a police raid on the house of the victim (Allen, 2015b).

Notes

1 www.liveleak.com/view?i=461_1434552519#9QU0QfUgty6eOPfW.99.
2 www.reddit.com/r/Adelaide/comments/3a0wqf/500_adelaide_women_fall_ victim_to_revenge_porn.
3 www.facebook.com/clementineford/posts/846206812123081:0.
4 This study was funded by the Australian Institute of Criminology and involved nine focus groups with young Australians aged 18–20 regarding their views on technology and sexuality. The focus groups ran for an average of 90 minutes and contained between three and ten participants with an average of seven. They were conducted at universities and adult education centres in inner city, outer suburb and rural locations in New South Wales, Australia.
5 www.statista.com/statistics/264810/number-of-monthly-active-facebook-users-worldwide.
6 www.statista.com/statistics/282087/number-of-monthly-active-twitter-users.
7 In fact, the 'screenshot' option on many phones enables users to capture and permanently store Snapshot images. Users have been able to use third-party applications to permanently save and store Snapchat images, although Snapchat recently put measures in place to stop this.
8 www.similarweb.com/website/reddit.com

Suggested links

Facebook: www.facebook.com.
Twitter: www.twitter.com.
Youtube: www.youtube.com.
Snapchat: www.snapchat.com.
Reddit: www.reddit.com.
4chan: www.4chan.org.
8chan: www.8chan.co.

1

TOWARDS A CRITICAL THEORY OF ONLINE ABUSE

Social media has an ambivalent place in public discourse. Over the last 10 years, it's been heralded as the augur of a new ethos of 'sharing' and sociality, trivialised as the playground of children and adolescents, demonised as the tool of paedophiles and terrorists, and credited with the overthrow of tyranny and revitalisation of political dialogue. This kaleidoscope of competing images is testament to the far-reaching implications of new media technologies, not the least of which is the challenge that it poses to established media interests. The rise of social media and an increasingly technology-savvy citizenry has undermined the business model of newspapers and television in particular. This has led to major falls in revenue as 'old' media reorientates itself, somewhat reluctantly, within a new technological landscape. Perhaps it is not surprising, then, that 'old' media has enthusiastically disseminated stories about the apparent threats the social media poses to social order and safety. 'Sexting', 'revenge porn', cyber-bullying, cyber-harassment, and online child exploitation are now familiar examples of the pitfalls of social media. However, populist presentations of online abuse as a new and pressing threat to children and young people can obscure the intersection of new technology with existing patterns of abuse and violence. Online abuse is underpinned by entrenched power differentials on the basis of gender, age and other factors, and 'crosses over' with 'offline' harms such as domestic violence, bullying and sexual harassment. Social media has come to saturate social life to such an extent that the distinction between 'online' and 'offline' abuse has become increasingly obsolete, requiring a nuanced understanding of the role of new media technologies in abuse, crime and justice responses.

The aim of this chapter is to provide a critical overview of the history of online abuse on social media and to propose a critical theory of online abuse that situates new technology within the power relations that shape its development and deployment. The chapter challenges the focus of public debate on the sexual victimisation of children by strangers on social media and foregrounds the ways in which online abuse has changed with the rise of social media platforms. Crucial to this discussion is the status of social media as a network of corporate platforms that profit from the commodification of user data. Communication on social media is induced by software architecture that actively encourages the publication and circulation of private, emotive or provocative material that drives market share and revenue. It is within the tension between communication and commodification that online abuse takes shape and meaning, and exerts its impacts on users and public debate. Avoiding simple dichotomies, the chapter recognises that social media can host meaningful interpersonal and political dialogue; however, the dynamics of commodification can encourage an instrumental attitude amongst users that is conducive to abuse and exploitation. The chapter draws on the traditions of critical theory to interrogate the place of online abuse within the forms of sociability enabled by social media, and the implications of social media for the circulation of claims of crime and injustice.

The history of abuse on social media

In the late 1990s, a number of high-profile internet companies and ventures failed when stock prices in the internet sector collapsed, leading to a prevailing sentiment that the potential for 'e-business' had been over-hyped. In 2005, publisher and internet commentator Tim O'Reilly began promoting what he called 'Web 2.0' as part of a concerted effort to identify viable online business strategies and resuscitate investor enthusiasm in the internet (O'Reilly, 2005). Web 2.0 described a new e-business model in which the online activities and interactions of users provide the content for web platforms and services, and generate data that could be monetised, usually by selling it to third parties and providing targeted advertising services. The search engine Google is one of the paradigmatic examples of the Web 2.0 model. It is an online-only service based on a vast dynamic database of information gleaned from other web pages, utilising a search algorithm that provides customised results to individual users (including targeted advertisements) (O'Reilly, 2005). Previously, software had usually been sold pre-packaged through retail outlets to be installed directly onto a computer. During this period, the online experience was characterised by web pages with limited interaction and a focus on conveying content to the reader. Web 2.0 was premised on applications and services that are only available online, often for free to the user, whose engagement with the service generates data that can be sold at a profit by the service (Gehl, 2012).

'Social media' describes those Web 2.0 applications that are specifically designed to facilitate interaction and communication between users. While arguably all media and technology is 'social' in the sense that they are produced and deployed within societies, Fuchs (2014b) characterises 'social media' platforms as specifically orientated towards enabling communication, collaboration and community-building. This is in contrast to earlier iterations of the internet in which the transmission of information was more static and less interactive, and more closely aligned with the 'broadcast' model of the mass media. With a critical mass of users, social media platforms provide fora for sustained patterns of communication between large numbers of people. The popularisation of social media has occurred contemporaneously with the proliferation of wireless access, and the convergence of camera, phone and internet technology on inexpensive mobile devices. This has gone some way to bridging class-based and global inequalities in internet and computer access, once referred to as the 'digital divide' (Norris, 2001), providing 'everyday' users with the ability to instantly transmit text, video and images to a global audience. Another consequential impact of social media is that it has proven particularly appealing to girls and women, driving an influx of female users into what had been previously a male-dominated internet (Ahn, 2011).

The first generation of social media sites emerged in the mid-to-late 1990s although many faltered due to design and technical faults, and the challenges of managing a large amount of user-generated content. For example, Friendster launched in 2002 and reportedly had over 3 million users within months (Rivlin 2006). A year after launch, Friendster declined an offer from Google to purchase the company for US$30 million (McMillan, 2013). The exponential growth of the site caused major engineering challenges. Slow loading times triggered vocal complaints from users (Chafkin, 2007). Once users had built their user profile, Friendster provided limited interactive opportunities and began to lose market share to emerging social media sites with more dynamic design features (Pachal, 2011).[1] From around 2004, the music-orientated Myspace emerged as the internationally dominant social media site. At least initially, Myspace was trumpeted as the realisation of the economic potential of Web 2.0. Myspace's user base grew exponentially within months of launching and the site was purchased by News Corp in 2005 for US$580 million dollars (Siklos, 2005). In 2006, Myspace registered its 100 millionth account (Adest, 2006) and, by 2007, the site was rumoured to have been valued at US$12 billion (Jackson, 2011).

By 2008, Myspace had entered into a steep decline as it began haemorrhaging users to rival Facebook, only to be sold for US$35 million to an advertising network in 2011 (Gehl, 2012). A number of explanations have been offered for the demise of Myspace, including the focus of News Corp on building the site's advertising revenue and a corresponding lack of innovation in enhancing and developing the Myspace platform (Chmielewski and Sarno, 2009). However, the risk of online abuse and crime had become a major public relations headache for the site. This was due in part to its roots in the indie rock and hip hop music scenes, which leant the site a visual style that was attractive to young people but largely alienated their parents (boyd, 2013). User profiles and conversations on Myspace frequently contained text and images with sexual content and references to drugs and violence (Moreno et al., 2009). This content was difficult if not impossible for Myspace to regulate given that Myspace profile pages were customisable to the point where users could rewrite its coding, so content was being generated in non-standardised ways across millions of profiles (Gehl, 2012). The subcultural look of the site, including the prevalence of sexualised and violent content, contributed to the view that it was unsafe. A largely overblown media narrative about 'online predators' and paedophiles on Myspace followed high-profile reporting of cases in which men lied about their age online in order to meet teenage girls for sexual activity (Marwick, 2008). In 2006, the suicide of US teenager Megan Meier, following harassment and abuse on Myspace from a user with a fake profile, contributed to growing concern about the vulnerability of young social media users (Gehl, 2012).

boyd (2013) has argued that the shift of users from Myspace to Facebook was analogous to the 'white flight' of the middle class to the suburbs and away from the poor and racialised communities of the inner city. In contrast to Myspace's origins in the music scene, Facebook originated as an Ivy League university social network, and built up a user base by expanding access to select universities and high schools over time. The 'elite' educational origins of the site appealed to middle-class parents and their children, in contrast to Myspace whose provocative displays of sexuality and racialised identity led to its stigmatisation as a 'ghetto' (boyd, 2013: 219). As users began to abandon Myspace, poor site security enabled fake and hacked profiles to proliferate, hosting malware, viruses and advertisements for pornography and dating sites. When combined with the often 'messy' look of Myspace profile pages, the site took on an increasingly abandoned and vandalised appearance (boyd, 2013). This only exacerbated the contrast with Facebook, whose promise of security and safety was reinforced by the site's clean visual interface, which involves highly standardised profile pages in contrast to Myspace's clutter. Facebook engages moderators to detect and remove material deemed inappropriate, such as nudity, sexually explicit or drug-related images or text (Chen, 2013, 2014), and actively seeks to ensure that profiles on the site are in the user's legal name. It also has a range of evolving response mechanisms to potential or identified threats to child safety on the platform. The clean, simple interface of Facebook and the regulation of identity and content has been important in quelling user anxiety and attracting a much broader demographic of social media users. It also reinforced the role of social media in building a public-facing 'self-brand' (Banet-Weiser, 2012: 81) through which users promote and display a respectable identity. Teenagers interviewed by Livingstone (2009: 106) felt that Facebook's streamlined templates were more mature and 'sophisticated' compared to Myspace customised profiles covered in 'flowers' and 'hearts' and 'glitter'.

Online abuse and the threat of solicitation and harassment by strangers have been important in shaping the contemporary social media landscape. It is perhaps ironic, then, that the rise of social media has coincided with a major drop in reports of online stranger harassment. Prior to social media, group online interaction occurred primarily on chat rooms and discussion boards that tended to facilitate communication between strangers. Research at the time suggested that a significant proportion of users in youth-orientated chat rooms and other online sites were adults misrepresenting themselves as teenagers in order to engage young users in sexualised interaction (Lamb, 1998). Chat rooms were a particularly common site for the sexual solicitation of children and young people by strangers (Mitchell et al., 2001). The shift to social media, which facilitates contact between users known to one another, has resulted in a significant decline in this activity. Large nationally representative surveys of young Americans aged 10–17 found that reports of unwanted online sexual solicitations online in the past year more than halved from 19 per cent in 2000 to 9 per cent in 2010 (Mitchell et al., 2013). The authors suggest that, 'rather than making youth more vulnerable, the social networking revolution may have provided an additional measure of protection' from unwanted sexual attention from strangers online (Mitchell et al., 2013: 1233).

The shift to social media has not eradicated online abuse, far from it. As stranger harassment has dropped, online sexual solicitations by those known to the child appear to have increased (Mitchell et al., 2013), and so too have reports of harassment by acquaintances involving threats or other offensive behaviours (Jones et al., 2013). Young people's use of social media is giving new shape and form to intimate coercion and sexual harassment. This effect is particularly acute for girls and young women, who are at disproportionate risk of humiliation and intimidation through online invasions of privacy (Salter, 2015). In high schools, sexual harassment can escalate with the collection and sharing of sexual or nude images of female classmates via social media and mobile phones (Ringrose et al., 2013). Similar patterns have been observed amongst adults, such as the case described in the Introduction, in which adult men circulated images of their ex-partner online. The use of social media to monitor and control partners or ex-partners (including releasing or threatening to release private images and video) is an increasingly common tactic amongst domestic violence perpetrators (Southworth et al., 2007). In these cases, the 'inward' turn of social media towards dense connectivity between known users effectively poisons the user's social world with defamatory or embarrassing online content. Public figures, particularly women and those from racial or sexual minority groups, report consistent abuse on social media in an effort to silence them and drive them from public debate. Misogyny, racism and other forms of prejudice often intersect in social media harassment.

The business model of Web 2.0 is founded on the largely unregulated generation of content by a mass of users. As a result, the internet is full of 'garbage', as technology journalist Sarah Jeong (2015) memorably put it: junk content ranging from abuse and threats to spam and viruses. A key question is: 'Who puts the garbage out?' That is, on a platform that generates profit by commodifying user-generated content, whose job is it to manage the risk of abusive content and minimise its harms? It is clear that certain types of 'garbage' trigger a prompt response from social media platforms. Having learnt from the fate of Myspace, social media platforms are highly responsive to concerns about child safety. So too are the police, to the point where a significant proportion of arrests for internet-facilitated sexual crimes against minors involve entrapment by a police officer posing online as a child (Mitchell et al., 2010). In contrast, women complaining of the non-consensual circulation of intimate images and threats of death and sexual violence on social media report little or no response from social media safety teams, while police are often disinterested or uncertain of how to respond (Salter and Crofts, 2015). With the 'staggering' number of reports of abuse on social media, US law enforcement representatives claim they are forced to triage only the most extreme cases, specifically those involving immediate risk of physical harm or threats to children (Hess, 2014). When it comes to the abuse of adults, the cooperation of social media sites with police investigations has been patchy at best, with sites keen to maintain the anonymity and confidentiality of their users. This position has become increasingly untenable as public attention focuses on the capacity of social media to host racist, neo-Nazi, Islamophobic, homophobic and misogynist groups and networks, and enable the coordination of campaigns of violence and intimidation. Understanding how social media facilitates and shapes abuse and prejudice is crucial to developing an adequate response.

Understanding the role of technology in online abuse

Implicit in debates over the potential harms and abuses of social media are a set of competing assumptions about the relationship between technology and society. This section outlines three general theoretical frameworks for understanding online abuse and critically evaluates their implications: utopian accounts of social media, dystopian accounts of social media, and instrumental accounts of social media. The utopian and dystopian approaches can be understood as substantive or determinist theories of technology, since they postulate that the architecture of the internet and social media necessarily generates specific kinds of identities, practices, relationships and societies. This has been a prominent strand of internet theorising. Since the internet was popularised in the mid-1990s, it was greeted as the architecture of a new form of human civilisation: an 'information society', 'communication society', 'network society', 'knowledge economy' or 'second modernity' characterised by increasingly sophisticated technological capabilities and networks. The *utopian account* celebrates this 'new' society or order as fundamentally positive, whereas the *dystopian account* suggests that the internet is pathological or anomic. This split reflects opposing portrayals of computer technology within the cultural imaginary as a medium for personal freedom and collective liberation on one hand, and an oppressive extension of government and corporate control on the other (Yar, 2014). This clash of values has been evident since the early days of computing and it persists in debates over online interaction and sociality. In contrast, the third approach, the *instrumental account*, posits that the internet is a neutral tool of human action. This approach generally focuses on human motivations for particular kinds of technological practice, while the material possibilities and histories of technologies are treated as secondary considerations if they are acknowledged at all.

Hand and Sandywell (2002) offer a useful distinction between 'strong' theoretical models that attribute intrinsic positive or negative properties to technologies, and 'weak' theoretical models in which technology is characterised as largely neutral, although likely to lend itself to particular ends. To a certain extent, utopian, dystopian and instrumental accounts of technology can be positioned on this spectrum, with 'strong' utopian and dystopian models at the far end, 'weaker' utopian and dystopian models in the middle, and instrumental accounts towards the 'weak' pole. In their descriptions of the effects of technology, these three accounts tend to assume some 'essence' to technology that is inherent to it or manifests in its application, lending themselves to specific responses and solutions. This section reflects on the underlying assumptions that inform debates on online abuse and proposed responses to it.

Utopian accounts of social media

Technological utopianism, the belief that technological progress is an inherently beneficial force, has been an important influence in debates over the internet and social media. It was a particularly prominent sentiment as social media was popularised in the mid-noughties. Theorists such as Jenkins (2006: 4) have embraced what he calls 'convergence culture', in which social media transforms consumers into media producers who are challenging media power structures. Bruns (2008: 2) identified social media users as newly empowered 'produsers'; that is, media consumers who had been transformed into producers and distributors, generating new models of participatory culture and politics. Other commentators propose that social media inaugurates an interlinked economic–political–social system, 'a new economic democracy...in which we all have a lead role' (Tapscott and Williams, 2008: 15). Shirky (2008: 172) has argued that social media literally creates 'freedom': social media 'creates what economics would call a positive supply-side shock to the amount of freedom in the world'.

The utopian perspective has articulated a range of potentials for personal and social benefit symbolised by social media. However, it has tended to blur the role of the social media user with capitalist consumer and demo-cratic citizen, suggesting in effect that the more closely these roles merge, the more 'empowered' the individual and the more robust the economic and political system. A particularly strong version of the utopian argument emerged in analyses of the 'Arab Spring' (a series of political uprisings in the Arab world beginning in 2011) and recent social movements that have been attributed in some quarters to the democratising power of social media. Castells (2012) made the argument that the Arab Spring 'emerged from calls from the Internet and wireless communication networks' (p. 106) and that the Occupy movement, a disparate social movement against transnational capitalism and corporate greed, 'was born on the Internet, diffused by the Internet, and maintained its presence on the Internet' (p. 168). These claims suggest that social media was the necessary precondition for political revival and appeals to the utopian sentiment that social media, by its very nature, is disseminating democratic thought around the globe.

Critics of the utopian position contend that it has ascribed social media an outsized position in contemporary history. In his detailed study of recent social and political movements, Gerbaudo (2012: 5) rejects emancipatory characterisations of social media as a form of 'fetishism'. He acknowledges social media's role in circulating compelling narratives and generating feelings of possibility that *may* be mobilised within public protest and collective action, but may also be dispersed and lost within the 'weak ties' that characterise social media. Likewise, in his study of the Occupy movement, Fuchs (2014a) recognised the opportunities that social media offers for social movements to publicise their cause, while emphasising the dangers posed by social media including 'surveillance, censorship, separation from street protests, infiltration by the police and secret services, corporate control and a stratified visibility and attention economy' (p. 126). It is clear that social media is not inherently democratic and can be repurposed for oppressive, fascist or even genocidal projects. Social media platforms such as Facebook and Twitter have emerged as powerful propaganda tools for radical extremist groups such as Islamic State/Daesh, who actively recruit new members on social media and use it to distribute horrific videos of their atrocities.

The utopian approach generally minimises the prevalence of online abuse and harm, characterising it as an infrequent byproduct of an otherwise beneficial technology. This ethos has been invoked by Web 2.0 entrepreneurs and social media companies to minimise their duty of care to users. When asked in 2009 about the privacy implications of Google, CEO Eric Schmidt infamously responded 'If you have something that you don't want anyone to know, maybe you shouldn't be doing it in the first place' (quoted in Esguerra, 2009). This was followed by statements from Facebook CEO Mark Zuckerberg that privacy is no longer a 'social norm', and that people are 'really comfortable' with sharing personal information widely on social media (Johnson, 2010). These quotes suggest that online abuse and invasions of privacy are either the fault of the victim or they are becoming less impactful over time, as society is transformed by the force of social media. Such sentiments have justified relatively limited responses to online abuse from social media platforms, such as various 'block' and 'report' options that allow users to avoid interaction with other users, or potentially report them to the platform and the authorities. However, as the next chapter demonstrates, these measures are easily circumvented by dedicated abusers, while users who are frequently targeted (due to their gender, race, sexuality or some other factor) can be overwhelmed by the burden of individually responding to each abuser. Meanwhile, users complain of inconsistent and delayed responses to abuse on social media platforms by moderators whose enforcement of the terms of service is often sporadic at best.

Dystopian accounts of social media

In contrast to utopian perspectives, dystopian accounts suggest that social media is inherently harmful or inevitably lends itself to misuse and abuse. The 'strong' variant of these claims include empirically dubious claims that social media induces mental illness, addiction and the destruction of mental faculties. Social media has been accused of permanently altering users' brains, generating impulsivity and a lack of empathy (Wintour, 2009), attention deficit disorder (Boddy, 2013), depression, addiction and suicidality (*Huffington Post*, 2013). A common allegation is that social media is unsuitable for physiologically immature 'adolescent brains' (Lovink, 2011: 19). Such descriptions of mental damage and decline correspond with cultural criticism that social media replaces the 'complex inner density' of intellectual accomplishment with shallow tendencies towards immediate gratification (Carr, 2008). Anxiety that social media is flattening out 'high' culture is repeated in warnings about 'mob rule' and 'digital Darwinism', in which only the 'loudest and most opinionated' survive (Keen, 2007: 15). A range of theorists and commentators argue that the internet is fragmenting public dialogue (Habermas, 2006), promoting political inconsequential forms of speech (Dean, 2010), and locking users into narcissistic 'filter bubble' of shared opinions and experiences (Pariser, 2011). Meanwhile, criminological and surveillance studies literature warns that the internet is creating a control society, a panopticon or a synopticon in which the internet features as a method of corporate control and authoritarian surveillance (e.g. McGuire, 2007).

These dystopian accounts recognise the power of technological systems to influence human action and extend oppressive forms of social control. However, technological dystopianism tends to overestimate the coherence and power of technological systems, and underestimates the capacity of users to engage with technology in a creative or subversive mode. The future of technology is not determined by itself but rather features as a contingent dimension of human praxis which shapes, but does not dictate, expressions of agency and resistance. Dyer-Witheford (1999) observed that a society that is pervaded by new media technology is not inevitably controlled by it. To the contrary, the pervasiveness of this technology has furnished entire populations with the technological literacy for a range of 'appropriations, counterplans and alternative logics' (Dyer-Witheford, 1999: 129). The very existence of online abuse is suggestive of continuing social conflict within social media rather than manufactured consensus.

Dystopian accounts of social media provide few solutions for online abuse other than the rejection of social media altogether, or the generation of new social media platforms free from corporate or government influence. The potentials of non-commodified and communitarian online platforms have been explored by political activists and researchers (Fuchs, 2014a). However, these alternatives do not address the problem of online abuse on social media as it occurs on mainstream and increasingly monolithic platforms. Van Dijck (2013) questions whether it is feasible to 'opt out' of large social media platforms given their central role in the organisation of personal and sometimes professional life. He observes that, for young people, '*not* being on Facebook means not being invited to parties, not getting updated on important events, in short, being disconnected from a presumably appealing dynamic of public life' (Van Dijck, 2013: 51). There is a growing list of professions where a presence on popular social media sites such as Twitter or LinkedIn is highly advantageous if not effectively compulsory: journalists, information technology professionals, games developers, academics, researchers, consultants, policy analysts and so on. Ultimately, the dystopian critique of technology is too indiscriminate to inform solutions to online abuse. Instead, this critique usually terminates 'in retreat from the technical sphere into art, religion or nature' (Feenberg, 1996: 26) as evidenced in romantic portrayals of a 'high' culture or more 'meaningful' communication supposedly endangered by social media.

Instrumental accounts of social media

In contrast to the two approaches just described, the instrumental view casts social media as a neutral phenomenon that can be put to a range of ends, good or bad. On the face of it, this approach appears relatively objective in that it avoids the pitfalls of technological determinism, and emphasises the responsibility of human agents in our use of social media. This approach resolves moral and ethical questions about the value of social media by focusing on how it is used by human beings. It is the preferred framework for social scientists, who are attracted to its ostensibly apolitical leanings, as well as software engineers and programmers focused on questions of efficiency and design rather than 'messy ideological disputes and inchoate values' (Pariser, 2011: 177). An instrumental view also validates the efforts of social media entrepreneurs to position their platforms as nothing more than neutral 'utilities'. Facebook frequently describes itself as a 'social utility', while Twitter co-founder Jack Dorsey said in 2009:

> I think Twitter's a success for us when people stop talking about it…and people just use it as a utility, use it like electricity. It fades into the background, something that's just a part of communication. We put it on the same level as any communication device. So, e-mail, SMS, phone. That's where we want to be.
>
> *(quoted in McCarthy, 2009)*

This presentation of Twitter as a 'utility' comparable to the electrical grid characterises the social media platform as a neutral facility that individuals use to meet their own needs. However, social media does not simply 'channel' user interaction but actively 'programs' the manner in which that interaction takes place (Van Dijck, 2013: 6). An orientation towards 'sharing' and publishing content, with an eye to commodifying that information in a variety of ways, is coded into social media platforms. The instrumental account not only makes invisible the economic imperatives that shape social media, but it tends to ignore other implicit power structures that have long shaped access to, and participation in, computing and information technology. The instrumental focus on 'efficiency' and 'design' as over-riding technological criteria for success has long sidelined concerns over the homosocial and often sexist milieus that characterise engineering and computing, and have become an embedded feature of online interaction (van Zoonen, 2002).

Feenberg (2002) argues that the instrumental view of technology is not as scientifically objective or politically unaffiliated as it appears. Instead it reflects the Western liberal view of the individual subject as a 'little god' who uses technology to exert his will on others and the world (Feenberg, 2002: 111). It assumes a high degree of rationality and premeditation on behalf of the individual user of technology that is congruent with the liberal model of the 'rational actor', in which human behaviour is primarily driven by calculations of risks and benefits. When applied to online crime, the 'rational actor' approach characterises perpetrators as motivated individuals who take advantage of the particular characteristics of the internet to commit their crimes. Insofar as social media is factored into this analysis, it is understood as a collection of technological capabilities (such as reach, speed and anonymity) that makes crime more or less likely. For example, during the London Riots of 2011, in which over 2,500 shops were looted over four days, UK politicians and journalists claimed that the reach and speed of Twitter, Facebook and mobile phones enabled 'thugs' and 'mobs' to organise riots and looting (Fuchs, 2014b: 201).

This is an impoverished account of online crime. The UK riots were triggered by the shooting death of a black man, Mark Duggan, by London police, and Winlow and colleagues (2015: 148) argue that the riots were symptomatic of a complex of inchoate anger and frustrated desire for consumer goods amongst disadvantaged groups otherwise excluded from the spectacle of consumption. Focusing on social media as the enabling factor in the riots eclipses the stark social realities that triggered them (Fuchs, 2012: 385). Moreover, abuse and harassment as it takes place online is often 'expressive' rather than 'acquisitive' (see Hayward, 2007 for further elaboration of this distinction), in the sense that it discloses and reveals emotional sentiments and subjective worldviews, rather than being motivated by a rational interest in gain or profit. This focus on motivated individual offenders not only provides a reductionist account of the complexity of online abuse but it resonates with a neoliberal carceral politics and exaggerated anxieties over online risks. Since it assumes that offenders can be deterred by increasing the likelihood and penalties of detection, instrumental logics reinforces punitive 'law and order' approaches to online crime, and endorses the use of surveillance and punishment to deter offenders. Narratives of the highly motivated and calculative 'cyber-terrorist' or 'online sexual predator' now feature prominently in the legitimisation of arguments for internet censorship, surveillance and data retention.

Fantasies of cyber-crime

All three approaches to online abuse – utopian, dystopian and instrumental – converge somewhat incoherently in the diverse literature on 'cyber-crime'. The term 'cyber-crime' was popularised by the mass media in the 1990s to describe crime that supposedly takes place in 'cyber-space' (Wall, 2001). As a moniker for online interaction, 'cyber-space' originates in the work of famous science fiction author William Gibson (1984) who described a three-dimensional computer-generated space in which data is graphically depicted and navigated. In many regards, 'cyber-space' captured the futurism of programmers and computer enthusiasts who claimed that computers could turn ordinary people into 'gods' (Turner, 2010: 82). The mystique cultivated by programmers as rulers of this 'new world' was a captivating one that came to circulate throughout pop culture and academia. The term suggests not only that the internet has the power to profoundly reshape the world, but that the internet itself *contains a new world*.

There is a range of problems with the 'cyber-crime' paradigm. The first and most obvious is that 'cyber-space' doesn't exist. In his novel, Gibson (1984: 67) called 'cyberspace' a 'consensual hallucination', and McGuire (2007) argues it has taken on hallucinatory qualities in the criminological literature on online crime as well. He provides an entertaining summary of the magical properties attributed to cyber-space by criminologists and other academics who adopt the language of both science fiction and religion to describe cyber-space as a transcendental, extra-dimensional universe (McGuire, 2007: 2–3, 21–22). The notion of the internet as a 'virtual' or parallel reality is a poor framework for understanding online interaction, and particularly so in the 1990s when 'cyber-crime' literature began to emerge. This was a period in which most internet communication took place on email, discussion boards and other text-based interfaces that were a far cry from the immersive digital world described by Gibson. Academics have had to take significant poetic license to bridge the gap between the so-called 'cyber-space' and the more mundane realities of user experience, often appealing to post-structuralist notions of the body and identity as text to ground fantasies of 'cyber-space' in some kind of semi-coherent framework.

Once its mystifying properties are set aside, the term 'cyber-crime' 'does not do much more than signify the occurrence of a harmful behaviour that is somehow related to a computer' (Wall, 2001: 2). This raises questions about the utility of 'cyber-crime' as a category or target of inquiry. The term can be used to group various grisly and unusual crimes – the German cannibal who met his consenting victim online, the man who abducted the 12-year old girl he groomed online via a chat room, and so on – with relatively common behaviours, such as online harassment, in a manner that does little to dispel the sensationalism around the issue (Jewkes, 2007). Prefixing various crimes with 'cyber' can inaccurately conflate physical offences with online abuse (e.g. 'cyber-rape' to describe threats of rape, 'cyber-violence' to describe online insults), creating unwieldy categories that lack critical purchase. For instance, a recent United Nations report used the umbrella term 'cyber-violence' to describe everything from hate speech and hacking to human trafficking and the advocacy of genocide (UN Women, 2015). Not only does 'cyber-violence' fail to recognise the different antecedents and sequelae of these diverse crimes, but it hinges on a metaphorical link to physical violence that does not attend to the specificity of online abuse.

The concept of the internet as 'cyber-space' or a 'virtual reality' is undoubtedly popular but it has a number of pernicious effects when applied to online abuse, beyond simply mischaracterising it. Idealisations of 'cyber-space' as the 'home of Mind' (Barlow, 1996: 11) or a 'networks of mind' (Castells, 2009: 137) in which users are disembodied from their everyday lives have contributed to trivialising portrayals of online abuse as occurring in a 'parallel' world without 'real' impact. This in turn has legitimised what Phillips (2015: 128) calls a colonialist mentality that seeks to 'invade' and 'conquer' other users and online platforms using any means necessary (Phillips, 2015: 129–130). She argues that the 'raids' and 'mob harassment' that are now common on social media are a perverse re-enactment of an American 'Wild West' ethos, reinforced by descriptions of the internet as a new and uncharted 'cyber' world. Far from describing online abuse, notions of 'cyber-space' and 'virtual reality' may inadvertently reinforce its legitimisation.

The proposition that the internet represents a portal into 'cyberspace', or the internet is blurring the real into the virtual (Aas, 2013), may have imbued academic inquiry into 'cyber-crime' with a certain gravity but at the cost of grasping more clearly how online abuse takes shape and exerts impacts on people's lives and society. Predicated on a division between 'online' and 'offline' worlds, this problematic artifice has become increasingly untenable in the age of social media and the 'internet of things' as online connectivity proliferates across multiple devices. Writing about online harassment, Cross (2014: 5) emphasises the 'reality' in 'virtual reality', as the internet confronts us 'not with a pure simulation, but a consequential social world whose vistas are expanding moment to moment'. Online abuse and its impacts flow into and beyond online platforms and require a contextualised understanding of technology and its role and function in the lives of users and societies.

A critical theory of online abuse

Utopian, dystopian and instrumental theories all address different dimensions of the technology–society relationship but none of them, alone, offers a comprehensive explanation of online abuse. Instrumental approaches tend to assume a rational individual actor who is motivated to commit online crime, which offers a reductive account of online crime that legitimises punitive measures of control and punishment. Nonetheless, instrumental approaches give greater credence to human agency and creativity than the determinative theories of utopianism or dystopianism, which ascribes a causal power to technology to produce particular kinds of social relations and human behaviour. These approaches fail to adequately distinguish between technologically mediated practices, whether harmful or beneficial, and the technology itself. Both instrumental and determinative approaches maintain a focus on the lived contexts and behaviours of internet users in a manner that is obfuscated by the unnecessary fiction of 'cyber-space'.

Critical theory offers an alternative theoretical resource for understanding the relationship between technology and society that takes account of historical and cultural context. The origins of critical theory lie with the Frankfurt School, a loosely affiliated group of twentieth-century social theorists and philosophers who offered a re-interpretation of Marxist theory with a focus on, amongst other things, the role of culture and technology in social change. The first generation of the Frankfurt School, which included figures such as Max Horkheimer, Theodore Adorno and Herbert Marcuse, combined macro-level sociological analyses with psychoanalytic theory to examine the relationship between media technologies, consumer society and the social ordering of lived experience. Adorno and Horkheimer developed an important critique of the industrialisation of cultural production (the 'culture industries'), in which they explained how the mass media stimulated needs and urges within audiences that cleaved them to lifestyles of mass consumption (Horkheimer and Adorno, 1972). In his account of a technologically rationalised society, Marcuse (1964) argued that technological systems instantiated with capitalist values were fundamentally reshaping subjectivity and human relations. The overall impression given by the early Frankfurt School thinkers was of a society in which the hegemony of the mass media and technological rationality was foreclosing opportunities for critical thought and resistance.

Subsequent scholars influenced by the Frankfurt School have sought to identify more expansive possibilities for human agency and democratic change. For these theorists, the relationship between technology, media and society is more unpredictable and open to transformation. Habermas's (1989) work on the 'public sphere' emphasised the egalitarian possibilities of collective debate and meaning-making, and the flow of democratic discourse from the intimate contexts of the family, to informal conversations and arguments, to decision-making bodies such as parliaments. He was critical of the interlocking of technological, political and corporate power in the mass media, but nonetheless argued that public democratic debate contained a utopian ideal of mutual equality between participants that could be excavated and realised. Against Habermas's (1989) description of a singular 'public sphere', Fraser (1990) and other theorists such as Warner (2002) have emphasised the dynamic pluralism of the public sphere in which subaltern voices have contested their exclusion and adopted modes of public representation outside the mass media. This has included the use of networked computing and internet technologies to circulate counter-hegemonic discourse to a wider audience. The potential role of the internet and social media in reviving the public sphere, and democratising access to it, has been the subject of speculation since the early 1990s, and this is discussed in more detail in the following chapter. For now, it's useful to recognise the increasingly central position of the internet and social media within the circulation of discourse within pre-existing 'publics' (for example, party politics, feminist groups, trade unions), as well as its role in the sponsoring of new 'publics' and the expansion of others that had previously been limited to smaller fora and alternative media.

Within a critical theory perspective, understanding the phenomenon of abuse on social media requires an appreciation of the technological conditions of its possibility; that is, the manner in which the design of social media interfaces and architecture makes online abuse possible and meaningful. Critical theory characterises technology as embedded within and expressive of the worldviews and systems in which it takes shape and is applied, while recognising that the application and impacts of technology are not pre-determined and features within social struggles over power and public representation. Online abuse can be situated within the objectifying technological rationality of social media insofar as, in their use of social media, users are induced to objectify their own and other's characteristics and enter into a competitive ranking system whereby their profiles and content are 'rated' by other users. As Chapter 3 argues in more detail, abuse and harassment reflects the objectifying and exploitative dimensions of this process and indeed can function as a successful strategy in garnering attention and cultural capital on social media. Meanwhile, social media companies and online platforms have an incentive *not* to intervene in online abuse, since abuse and controversy can generate a high volume of traffic and therefore profit, while content regulation and moderation is expensive.

As they intersect with existing inequalities within peer groups and social contexts, the objectifying tendencies of social media can amplify or create new iterations of abuse and harassment while radically limiting the options available for the targets of abuse. Chapters 4 and 5 argue that inducements towards visibility and exposure on social media intersect with entrenched sexist double standards that can vigorously sanction the online displays of girls and women. Nonetheless, the instantiation of technological design with specific values and their correspondence with broader patterns of social conflict do not completely determine user behaviour or experience. New contexts and patterns of technological application can produce unexpected and confounding effects, including the generation of norms and values that reshape how technology is developed and applied. In the case of media technology, this impacts on how social issues such as crime and abuse are framed, interpreted and responded to. Chapter 6 in this book identifies how the transnationalisation of discourses of crime and justice via social media can generate unexpected and radical insights into social problems.

This recursive relationship between new media technology, society, users and discourses of crime and justice has often been overlooked in efforts to reduce technological harms. While the Frankfurt School foregrounded important social, historical and political considerations in the society–technology relationship, its analysis doesn't allow for sufficient specificity regarding particular forms of technology such as social media, and tends towards pessimism and retreatism in its account of public discourse. Meanwhile, contemporary studies into forms of online abuse such as non-consensual 'sexting' and 'revenge porn' have generally focused on the need for legal regulation, the motives of those who engage in these harms and the impacts on victims, while overlooking the role of social media platforms and other technological media in giving shape and form to relations of abuse and exploitation, or sponsoring new discourses and reactions to abuse. Understanding and responding to online abuse requires a more fine-grained study of social media attuned to its specific socio-technical configurations, and how these shape and are shaped by diverse contexts, patterns of use and discourses of crime and justice.

Conclusion

Complaints of abuse and harassment on social media have grown to the point where they can no longer be minimised or dismissed. It has become apparent that abuse and harassment is a predictable and recurring feature of social media rather than just a 'glitch' or 'bug'. This is now being acknowledged by social media companies. As Twitter CEO Dick Costolo stated to employees in a leaked internal memo 'We suck at dealing with abuse and trolls on the platform and we've sucked at it for years' (quoted in Tiku and Newton, 2015). As the full scale of online abuse becomes apparent, debates over the appropriate response reveal a lack of consensus over precisely how technology impacts on society or the appropriate response. This chapter endorses a critical theoretical framework utilising a dialectical approach that recognises the potentials *and* pitfalls of social media. Online abuse is not an inevitable feature of social media, nor the 'fault' of particular types of individuals or systems, but rather it can be situated within the contradictory dynamics at work on social media and in society at large. As this book will go on to examine, multiple forces contribute to online abuse, including the profiteering of social media companies, the perpetuation of hegemonic formulations of 'public' and 'private' life, the normalisation of misogyny within online networks and computer-related industries, and routine sexual harassment and coercion in peer and intimate contexts. Social media has provided new discursive opportunities to renegotiate what is 'public' and what is 'private' as well as who gets to speak in 'public' and what they can say. These opportunities can be abused in ways that perpetuate existing inequalities but they can also be appropriated to circumvent oppressive arrangements and expand the scope for speech and action. The next chapter will discuss in more detail how social media is reconfiguring understandings of privacy and publicity and its implications for struggles over crime and justice.

Note

1 With a major decline in user traffic in the United States but steady interest from Asian users, Friendster was sold in 2009 and relaunched as a 'social gaming' site based in Malaysia.

Suggested links

Myspace was redesigned and relaunched in 2013 to mixed reviews. See the new site at https://myspace.com.

Journalist Adrian Chen (Twitter: @AdrianChen) wrote an in-depth piece on the outsourcing of social media content moderation to developing countries at: www.wired.com/2014/10/content-moderation.

Read sociologist P.J. Rey's (Twitter: @pjrey) account on the 'myth of cyberspace' at http://thenewinquiry.com/essays/the-myth-of-cyberspace.

You can find the Stanford Encyclopedia of Philosophy's entry on the Frankfurt School at: http://plato.stanford.edu/entries/critical-theory.

2

GAMERGATE AND THE SUBPOLITICS OF ABUSE IN ONLINE PUBLICS

 Zoë "Shitpost" Quinn
@UnburntWitch

When online abuse becomes prolific to a certain point, it becomes the background hum of your life and you have to live it differently.

RETWEETS	LIKES
72	126

2:55 AM - 4 Aug 2015

FIGURE 2.1

This chapter opens with a tweet from Zoe Quinn (Figure 2.1), video game developer and one of the primary targets of a ferocious campaign of online abuse known as Gamergate. As Quinn's tweet suggests, she is amongst a number of other women targeted by Gamergate to the point where online abuse has become the 'background hum' of their lives, which they are now forced to live 'differently'. Gamergate was the culmination of a series of incidents within the gaming industry, and in the field of informational technology more generally, indicative of the misogynist hostility that has greeted the perceived 'intrusion' of women and more diverse users. Through an analysis of Gamergate, the chapter emphasises the political dimensions of online abuse as a perpetuation of the exclusion of groups that have typically been unwelcome in the public sphere. The particular technical affordances of online platforms are inextricably bound up with such collective projects of abuse in the way that they sponsor cultures and practices of harassment while inhibiting victim or bystander intervention.

The chapter begins with an examination of the political relevance of the public/private divide before applying it to the internet and social media, focusing in particular on the culture of anonymous online sociality sustained by 4chan, Reddit and 8chan and their clash with the heterogeneous publics of social media. The chapter emphasises how the misuse of personal and private information, so central to online abuse, is made possible through the technological configurations of social media, against a backdrop of stigma and discrimination in which the personal information of subordinate groups is particularly vulnerable to misappropriation. Drawing on Beck's (1997) notion of the 'subpolitical', the chapter characterises Gamergate as structured by an implicit politics of aggrieved masculine entitlement and sexism. While highly personal, online abuse is also fundamentally political, and suggestive of an ongoing struggle for control and dominance within online publics.

Publicity, privacy and abuse

As concepts, publicity and privacy are the focus of a multitude of overlapping and somewhat conflicting associations. Weintraub (1997) identifies two meta-theoretical themes in approaches to the public/private divide across politics, law, sociology, anthropology and feminist theory. He suggests, first, that the public/private distinction is used to refer to that which is 'hidden or withdrawn versus what is open, revealed, or accessible' and second to 'what is individual…versus what is collective' (Weintraub, 1997: 5). These two points intersect to the extent that what is visible is typically visible to a collective. Personal or private life is associated with the world of families and domesticity while public life is understood as the place of collective sociability and government (Weintraub, 1997: 35). The market economy sits unevenly across the public–private divide as a matter for 'private' individuals and corporations but also a 'public' structure, in the sense that it is collective and politically consequential. The uncertain public or private status of the market economy reflects different theoretical approaches to the public/private divide, but, from a critical point of view, it underscores the pervasiveness of the market economy in both public and private life.

In liberal democracies, information, people and events usually become public or visible through the mass media, such as newspapers, television or radio. Ideally, the public circulation of information and discourse generates what Habermas (1989) called a 'public sphere', 'where such a thing as public opinion can be formed' (cited in McKee, 2004: 4). In critical theory, the public sphere describes a democratic ideal in which private citizens come together to collectively scrutinise the workings of the state and other authorities, generating points of consensus which then feed back into formal decision-making processes. Habermas (1989) took a generally pessimistic view of the critical potential of the contemporary public sphere in light of the commercialisation of the mass media. Unlike the more dispersed print culture that preceded it, the production and distribution of content to a mass audience through technologies such as television involve immensely expensive technologies that centralised ownership and control in corporate and state hands (Habermas, 1989: 187). Habermas (1989) argued that 'private' media ownership led to the degradation of the 'public sphere', since the mass media represented the interests of its elite owners and manipulated, rather than facilitated, the formation of public opinion.

The manner in which elite control of processes of cultural production reinforces social inequalities was famously described by Gramsci (1971) as 'hegemony', or a form of 'rule by ideas'. It is not simply that elites consciously promulgate media content that is advantageous to their interests and agendas, but also that their cultural dominance ensures that the most available modes of thought and understanding implicitly reinforce the status quo. This is sustained by the selective inclusion of specific voices and content in processes of media production and distribution, and by the exclusion of contradictory perspectives. Little wonder that participation in public life has been a major goal of oppressed

groups, such as the working class, women, and racial and sexual minorities, who have often generated their own means of publicity in the
form of alternative media. These groups have contested the excision of
their needs and concerns from public life, and drawn attention to the
exploitation and violence that arises from an excess of secrecy and
privacy. Scholars have identified the formation of a multiplicity of 'sub-
publics' (Warner, 2002) or 'counter-publics' (Fraser, 1990) that circulate
counter-hegemonic discourse and represent the needs of marginalised
groups. McKee (2004) uses the examples of the women's movement
and gay liberation to show how smaller 'publics' can, over time, have a
major impact on national and international discourse. This has included
redefining 'private' matters such as domestic violence or sexual orientation as publicly relevant, while contesting discrimination and bias in
the public sphere (Fraser, 1990).

Abuse remains a powerful force in curtailing the public activities of
subordinate groups. The personal characteristics of subordinate groups
are typically stigmatised within systems of hegemony, rendering the
subordinate vulnerable to public shame and humiliation in ways that
cannot be set in train so easily for those in positions of structural or
cultural advantage. For example, calling public attention to a white
person's race or a heterosexual person's sexual practices does not have
the equivalent impact of focusing on a black person's blackness, or a
gay man's participation in gay sex. As Goffman (1963) says, stigma
adheres more strongly to the powerless. Simply invoking and sexualising
a woman's gender in the form of common insults ('slut', 'bitch' and so
forth) is a well-recognised strategy to put the target 'in her place'; that
is, out of the public domain and in private life where she supposedly
belongs (Jane, 2014). Publicising stigmatising characteristics is not only
intimidating, and potentially a catalyst of prejudice or violence, but it
undermines the public standing of the target by denying the general
validity of their opinions and instead 'particularising' their views as partial
and inconsequential. This is in contrast to the characteristics of dominant
groups, such as wealthy white heterosexual men, whose personal attributes
are so expected in public life as to escape comment.

In summary, the construction of publicity and privacy map across
existing inequalities and can be actively turned against the powerless in the
maintenance of the status quo. The right to a private life, and to public

participation, is understood as fundamental to human flourishing in liberal democracies; however, the boundaries between the public and private are not equally advantageous. Subordinate groups may find themselves confined in the private sphere, unable to access public life and vulnerable to interpersonal violence and exploitation. When they enter public space and dialogue, they may find their privacy invaded and their personal characteristics used to legitimise insults and threats. The personal attributes of groups that have traditionally dominated public life generally fade into the background as expected and uncontroversial aspects of public figures, and hence they enjoy a relative degree of immunity from such strategies of abuse and vilification. This asymmetry in power enables prevalent but disavowed practices of abuse. Such abuse takes many forms but its overt public manifestations in the mass media are somewhat prescribed by journalistic codes of ethics, as well as the development of defamation, libel, confidentiality, anti-discrimination and civil or human rights laws, which provide some limits to outright public expressions of hate or aggression. Hence explicit abuse has operated more often on the periphery of public life as a common but disavowed regulatory mechanism that expresses the welcomeness of subordinate groups in public life. The next section argues that, as the internet expands access to the means of publicity and circumvents institutionalised forms of regulation, abuse has become a resurgent strategy through which to resist social transformation and reassert hegemonic ideologies of publicity and privacy.

The public sphere goes online

A range of concerns have been raised about the quality of the contemporary public sphere, including Habermas's (1989) charge that it is overly commercialised, and related criticisms that it is trivialising, fragmented and produces an apathetic polity (McKee, 2004). In the wake of these pessimistic assessments, the potential of the internet to enliven and reinvigorate the public sphere has been the subject of considerable interest. As the internet was being popularised, Keane (1995: 1) argued that:

> The old hegemony of state-structured and territorially-bounded public life mediated by radio, television, newspapers and books is being rapidly eroded. In its place are developing a multiplicity of

networked spaces of communication which are not tied immediately to territory, and which irreversibly fragment anything resembling a single, spatially-integrated public sphere with a nation-state framework.

These themes recur in largely positive accounts of the internet as a 'public sphere' or a contributor to the democratic process throughout the 1990s. In particular, the circumvention of state bureaucracy, the challenge to corporate control, the transnationalisation of communication, and the diversification of public dialogue were all identified as possible or likely outcomes of the dissemination of internet technology. Key to the political appeal of the internet is its potentially disruptive implications for the public/private divide, including its capacity to enable 'privatised' voices to become public. Researchers emphasised the critical potential of online discourse although they recognised persistent inequalities in access and unequal power in online communication (e.g. Schneider, 1996; Poster, 1997; Dahlberg, 2001).

The majority of 'early adopters' of computer technology and internet access in the 1980s and 1990s were young, white, heterosexual men in the Global North, reflecting the demographics of the information technology and engineering sectors more broadly (Kendall, 2000). A 'geek' variant of masculinity coalesced around computing technology during this period, in which technical mastery came to serve as an alternative foundation for masculine identity. This identity was actively defended on the internet against the perceived encroachment of women and other diverse users into online discourse. Researchers documented uneven but systemic patterns of aggressive discourse that intimidated and silenced women and other groups online (Herring, 1999; Sussman and Tyson, 2000; Morahan-Martin, 1998). This hostility could manifest in visceral forms, such as an infamous 1993 'virtual rape' incident when one anonymous participant in a multi-player online environment graphically described his character raping two other characters (Dibbell, 1993). The persistence of misogyny online reflects a long-standing tradition whereby women are dissuaded from public participation by threats of sexual violence and harassment (Valentine, 1989).

Male dominance of online communication has come under challenge by social media, which triggered a significant influx of women, children, racial and sexual minorities into these 'networked publics' (boyd, 2014). Even as numbers of social media users have exponentially increased, older and more exclusive patterns of online homosociality have been sustained by 4chan, 8chan and Reddit, in which participation is typically anonymous/pseudonymous and characterised by virulent sexism, racism and homophobia. Auerbach (2012) warns that users entering into these boards are:

> likely to witness a nonstop barrage of obscenity, abuse, hostility, and epithets related to race, gender, and sexuality ('fag' being the most common, often prefaced with any trait, e.g. 'oldfag,' 'straightfag'). Anyone objecting to this barrage will immediately attract a torrent of even greater abuse.

Coleman (2014: 40) described the use of shocking and offensive language on 4chan as 'a discursively constructed border fence meant to keep the uninitiated...far, far away'. The anonymity and ephemerality evident on the 'chan' image boards, where old messages and conversations are automatically deleted to make way for new threads, contributes to a lack of seriousness evident in much of this rhetoric of insult and abuse (Allen, 2014). However, this abuse is not indiscriminate but is largely directed at 'people of colour, especially African Americans, women, and gay, lesbian, bisexual transgender and queer (GLBTQ) people' (Phillips, 2015: 25). This functions to recentre the white, heterosexual male as the assumed subject of online participation while drawing on the specific characteristics of other groups to mark them out as marginal or indeed unwelcome.

Massanari (2015) observes how 'toxic' cultures and discourses of masculinity are 'enabled and propagated' by the 'chan' boards and Reddit, flowing across other online platforms such as social media. Far right political mobilisation is evident on 4chan boards such as /pol/ (the 'politically incorrect' board) well known for its advocacy of white supremacy and misogynist anti-feminism. Reddit is more closely moderated but nonetheless it continues to host extremist content. Reddit's numerous 'subreddits' includes the 'breakfeminazis' board, which hosts pornographic images and stories about the enslavement and rape of feminist women, as well as neo-Nazi content hosted on various racist subreddits including 'Coontown', which distributes videos in which black men are murdered in a variety of ways. Within these hives of reactionary prejudice, campaigns of abuse and harassment can be formulated and then rolled out, typically on social media. For example, in 2014, 4chan users conspired to set up large numbers of 'sockpuppet' (fake) Twitter accounts claiming to be feminists who wanted to 'end fathers' day' as a 'patriarchal' institution. These sockpuppet accounts spread the Twitter hashtag #endfathersday in an attempt to characterise feminist politics as extreme and out of touch (Alfonso III, 2014). This is just one of a number of so-called 'false flag' operations undertaken by 'channers' in an effort to infiltrate and undermine progressive social movements.

One of the most recent and well-known examples of such abuse campaigns was Gamergate, in which factions of 'hardcore' video game players conspired on 4chan and Reddit (and, later, 8chan) to drive prominent women from the video game industry and social media. Gamergate demonstrates the political force of personal insult and attack in efforts to control a vital media industry and indeed the publicity of social media itself, in which the architecture and lax administration of various online platforms is capitalised upon by large numbers of abusive users for maximum impact.

Gamergate

The term 'Gamergate' describes a shifting set of controversies played out online within the gaming industry and the broader 'gamer' community. It is difficult to provide a definitive history or overview to Gamergate which has unfolded based on loose affinities between thousands of online participants united in their defence of so-called 'gamer' culture.[1] In an interview, Chris Grant, editor-in-chief of video games website Polygon, explained the difficulties of trying to report on Gamergate:

> The closest thing we've been able to divine is that it's noise. It's chaos. And all you can do is extract patterns from the chaos. With no leaders, with no agenda, with no message, all you can do is find patterns. And ultimately Gamergate will be defined – I think has been defined – by some of its basest elements.
>
> *(Grant quoted in Ip, 2014)*

The recurrent themes within Gamergate social media activity are frustration over the perceived impingement of progressive politics into the video game industry, and the right of 'gamers' to enjoy gaming free from criticism about sexism, racism and homophobia. To legitimise this frustration, Gamergate has developed a constantly proliferating set of justifications whose logic is somewhat incoherent outside of 'gamer' subculture, ranging from complaints about unethical conduct in video games journalism to conspiracy theories about mass collusion between feminists, journalists and video game developers.

Before describing Gamergate, a brief overview of the video game industry is required. While often dismissed as 'just for kids', video and computer gaming is one of the most lucrative media industries in the world, with one market research firm estimated global games sales of US$91.95 billion in 2015 including console, PC and mobile phone games (Gaudiosi, 2015). As video and computer gaming developed in the 1990s, a focus on the presumptive young, male, heterosexual consumer was evident in games characterised by explicit violence and hyper-gendered presentations of masculine male fighters and large-breasted, often disposable female characters (Lien, 2013). Condis (2015) emphasised how these marketing assumptions transformed gaming into a media environment in which female and racial or sexual minority players have been marginalised, and discriminatory practices and language have been fostered. Although 'gamer' culture and the gaming industry is dominated by those men to whom the industry has primarily catered (Shaw, 2012), gaming is imagined in 'gamer' culture as a politically neutral, disembodied and transcendent pursuit in which the determining criterion for success is skill (Condis, 2015). This belies the vernacular of sexist, racist and homophobic abuse that is endemic in online and networked gaming and in gamer culture more broadly (Nakamura, 2014).

There have been major shifts in the video game industry over the last 10 years. The development of new consoles and the expansion of gaming to mobile phones and other platforms have drawn in female gamers in large numbers (Consalvo, 2012). Quantitative research suggests that players now have a relatively diverse gender, race and sexuality profile, including equal representations of male and female players (for a summary of recent surveys, see Nakamura, 2014). Increasingly inexpensive and sophisticated computer technology has enabled many players and fans to also become games developers, creating independent or 'indie' games with novel themes and sentiments that reflect the increasing diversity of players and developers. Major gaming studios are responding to their expanding consumer base by incorporating gay, lesbian and transgender storylines into their games alongside less stereotypical portrayals of women and racialised characters. These changes have been widely reported on by the 'indie' gaming blogs and websites that have developed as alternative sites of commentary to the more established gaming press, which has been criticised for its financial dependence on the gaming industry. These changes have been poorly received by gamers who view the new diversity of players, developers and media outlets as a threat to their subculture (Condis, 2015). Gender became a major fault line in this conflict. Women's rising profile in gaming has corresponded with an apparent intensification in gendered abuse and harassment from gamers over a number of years (Nakamura, 2014; Cross, 2014).

This abuse became particularly intensive and semi-coordinated in late 2014, producing a mass online movement of gamers and their allies that would come to be known as Gamergate. The trigger point for Gamergate was an embittered article posted online on 16 August 2014 by video game developer Eron Gjoni regarding his ex-girlfriend, the video game developer Zoe Quinn. Quinn is an 'indie' developer whose 2013 game *Depression Quest* had attracted award nominations and positive attention as well as a backlash from 'gamers'. *Depression Quest* depicted the experience of depression from a first person perspective, and involved a relatively simple text-based interface. The game symbolised a politically aware sentiment that prioritised narrative and character development over the graphical spectacle and technological skill valued in gamer culture by gamers. *Depression Quest* was met with hostility by gamers who alleged that 'political' games were infiltrating and supplanting gamer culture. Quinn was subsequently doxed and she began receiving rape threats at her home address and on the telephone (Kotzer, 2014). The abuse focused specifically on derogating Quinn's gender and sexuality, as well as her own well-known struggles with depression and suicidality. Quinn was outspoken about the abuse she was receiving, documenting and distributing evidence online and speaking to the gaming media about its impact on her. Her active resistance appeared to further infuriate her harassers. At the peak of the harassment, Quinn left her house and began living with friends to stay safe (Parkin, 2014).

This abuse campaign was already still simmering when Quinn ended her brief relationship with Gjoni. Gjoni retaliated by posting an article online claiming that Quinn had been unfaithful to him with other men in the gaming industry, including games journalist Nathan Grayson who worked for the 'indie' gaming site Kotaku. Gjoni's post was a compendium of details and inferences extracted from Quinn's social media profiles, mobile phone and email accounts (Jason, 2015). The clear inference of Gjoni's article was that Quinn's success as a developer was due to sexual favours. Gjoni went to considerable lengths to promote his article on platforms such as 4chan and Reddit frequented by gamers already hostile to Quinn. He did this in the apparent knowledge that Quinn would be likely subject to abuse. In a Twitter post on 28 August, he 'set the odds of [Quinn's] harassment at 80%'.[2]

Gjoni's article would have extraordinary ramifications. In the misogynist depths of Reddit and the various 'chan' boards, Quinn was emblematic of the manipulative femme fatale of feverish gamer imagination who was imposing 'politics' on the supposedly neutral meritocracy of gaming. Gjoni's post provided the 'smoking gun' that they had been looking for to establish that women's increasing prominence in gaming was undeserved and the result of sexual 'collusion' and journalistic 'corruption'. Gjoni actively encouraged gamers to expand their hostility to Quinn to encompass the 'journalism thing'; that is, his inference that Quinn slept with Grayson in exchange for favourable coverage. In a Reddit post on 25 August 2014, he recommended to redditors:

> Go focus on the journalism thing for a while. You don't even need to mention her name to address that issue. Come back to the Zoe thing after the vitriol dies down if you care about it.[3]

The suggestion that Grayson positively reviewed *Depression Quest* in exchange for sexual favours was quickly disproven, since Grayson had never written a review of Quinn's game. This proved irrelevant to the large numbers of gamers already uncomfortable with changes to the gaming industry. Their fears of an outright attack on gamer subculture were further inflamed by a series of articles in gaming websites encouraging the industry to orientate away from 'angry young men' as the paradigmatic video game consumer (e.g. Alexander, 2014). Under the banner of 'ethics in gaming journalism', gamers began a coordinated campaign of abuse and harassment targeting those who were critical of abuse and harassment in gaming, with a particularly intensive focus on Quinn and other prominent women in the industry.

The movement became known as 'Gamergate' on 27 August when actor Adam Baldwin, well known for his right wing views, tweeted a link to YouTube videos containing conspiratorial and defamatory claims about Quinn. This tweet included, for the first time, the hashtag #Gamergate, the suffix '-gate' signifying that the allegations against Quinn were indicative of a broader political scandal or conspiracy a la Watergate. Baldwin would later claim that 'leftists' with a 'totalitarian impulse' were trying to impose their 'political crap' on 'gamers' as part of a 'culture war' (Kaufman, 2014). Baldwin's intervention proved to be decisive. The hashtag #Gamergate was quickly adopted and spread by his 188,000+ Twitter followers.

Prior to the advent of Gamergate, Quinn's digital records of the online abuse and threats directed at her came to 16 megabytes. By December 2015, within just four months of Gamergate, she had reportedly logged 1,000 times this amount (Jason, 2015). Her Wikipedia entry was altered to record her death at the date of her next scheduled public appearance, and she began to receive thousands of death and rape threats on social media (Jason, 2015). One anonymous 4chan commentator threatened to 'give her a crippling injury that's never going to heal' the next time Quinn attended a gaming conference (Parkin, 2014). When she was doxed again, and her home address and contact details were released online, Quinn was forced to leave her house and stay with friends for six months (Jason, 2015). Her family also reported harassing phone calls. Gjoni publicly denied that he was encouraging the abuse and harassment of his ex-partner, but when solicited on Twitter by a user to participate more directly in her abuse, he stated 'I am actually doing a lot more than you know in the background' (Figure 2.2).

Quinn continued to actively document and publicise the orchestration of her harassment. She monitored the 'chan' boards and used her

FIGURE 2.2

Twitter and Tumblr (another micro-blogging social media site) accounts to distribute evidence that the campaign against her was pre-planned and coordinated. Her screenshots established that the Gamergate rationale of 'ethics in gaming journalism' was a deliberate confabulation invented on 4chan to deflect criticism away from their ongoing abuse of Quinn (McNally, 2014). In a Tumblr post, she wrote:

> The idea that I am required to debunk a manifesto of my sexual past written by an openly malicious ex-boyfriend in order to continue participating in this industry is horrifying, and I won't do it. It's a personal matter that never should have been made public, and I don't want to delve into personal shit, mine or anyone else's, while saying that people's love and sex lives are no one's business. **I'm not going to talk about it. I will never talk about it. It is not your goddamned business**.
>
> . . .
>
> This is another example of gendered violence, whereby my personal life becomes a means to punish my professional credentials and to try to shame me into giving up my work. (Emphasis in original.)[4]

In this compelling counter-narrative, Quinn argued, first, that Gjoni's article and its utilisation by Gamergate supporters constituted an extraordinary invasion of her privacy and, second, that this was a collective project of gendered abuse that aimed to force her and other women from the industry. She identified the way in which personal and private information about her was being publicised (regardless of its veracity) in a specifically gendered manner, foregrounding questions of sexuality and morality in way that is particularly humiliating to women. Meanwhile, Gjoni's conduct in compiling and distributing his post about her went entirely unscrutinised by Gamergate, a telling oversight for a movement claiming that their sole concern was 'ethical conduct' in the gaming industry. Quinn's protests and the evident hypocrisies and contradictions evident in Gamergate brought considerable negative mass media attention to the movement. In September 2014, discussion of Gamergate was banned from 4chan ostensibly for violating its (poorly enforced) rules against harassment, and migrated to 8chan, another image-board site known to host more extremist content (Howell O'Neill, 2014).

Although orchestrated anonymously on the 'chan' boards and other platforms such as Reddit (particularly the subreddit KotakuInAction), Twitter emerged as the main battleground of Gamergate. At its peak, the hashtag #Gamergate was used hundreds of thousands of times per month, and the majority of these mentions were in support of Gamergate. Those who used the hashtag to criticise Gamergate could be flooded for days or weeks with insults and threats. As technology designer Caroline Sinders (2015) observed:

> Using the hashtag in a tweet became akin to saying 'Bloody Mary' three times in a mirror, except Bloody Mary actually showed up and she brought a bunch of friends. People, particularly women in games, couldn't talk about Gamergate publicly without getting harassed, so they just stopped talking about it on Twitter.

The architecture of Twitter was highly conducive to this campaign of mass abuse and harassment. While Twitter provides an option that enables one user to 'block' another from interacting with them, this feature was rendered useless by Gamergate as it was not feasible to individually block hundreds or thousands of persistent abusers. In 2013, in response to a series of rape and death threats against high-profile women on the service, Twitter gave more prominence to their 'report' function enabling users to report 'abusive behaviour'. However, users have found that Twitter's safety team did not view explicit threats of rape, death or blackmail as a violation of their terms of service (West, 2014). Even where persistent abusers were suspended or banned, it was relatively quick and easy for them to create a new 'burner' account solely for the purpose of continuing the abuse. The unusually high prevalence of new Twitter accounts using the Gamergate hashtag suggested that supporters were creating large numbers of fake or 'sock-puppet' accounts to inflate their online presence and circumvent Twitter's anti-abuse measures (Johnston, 2014; Baio, 2014).

In late 2014, a range of developers and journalists who spoke up to defend Quinn and reject the sentiments of Gamergate were subject to doxing, hacking and serious abuse. After Quinn's friend and games developer Phil Fish tweeted in support of her, his website and social media accounts were hacked by a group of 4chan users, who referred to it as a 'public execution' of Fish for his 'feminist SJW [social justice warrior] tendencies' (Romano, 2014).[5] Notable Gamergate targets include games designer and journalist Jenn Frank, victimised for writing a piece in *The Guardian* about the harassment of women in games (Frank, 2014). Her harassment intensified to the point where she left the gaming industry, stating in one tweet on 4 September 2014 'Leave me alone, please, oh god, please'. On the same day, media critic and games designer Mattie Brice also announced she was distancing herself from the games industry due to harassment (Cox, 2014). In October, games developer Brianna Wu called the police and was forced to flee her home after receiving death and rape threats from a Twitter account called 'Death to Brianna' who also published her address. These threats followed a series of tweets from Wu mocking Gamergate. Wu provided a screenshot of these threats in a tweet that included the sardonic comment 'Remember, #gamergate isn't about attacking women' (Figure 2.3).

In the same month, cultural critic Anita Sarkeesian was forced to cancel a presentation at Utah State University after the school received anonymous threats of violence, including one that claimed affiliation with Gamergate, and another that alluded to the 1989 anti-feminist mass shooting at a Canadian university (Alberty, 2014). In early 2015, 8chan's /baphomet/ board organised for false tips to be sent to police about three critics of Gamergate, whose homes were raided by law

Brianna Wu
@Spacekatgal

 Follow

The police just came by. Husband and I are going somewhere safe.

Remember, #gamergate isn't about attacking women.

 @spacekatgal You just made a shitty game nobody liked. That's it. Nobody will care when you die.

 Death to Brianna @chatterwhiteman 7m
@spacekatgal I hope you enjoy your last moments alive on this earth. You did nothing worthwhile with your life.

 Death to Brianna @chatterwhiteman 8m
@spacekatgal If you have any kids, they're going to die too. I don't give a fuck. They'll grow up to be feminists anyway.

 Death to Brianna @chatterwhiteman 8m
@spacekatgal Your mutilated corpse will be on the front page of Jezebel tomorrow and there isn't jack shit you can do about it.

 Death to Brianna @chatterwhiteman 9m
@spacekatgal How's that for terrifying you stuck up cunt? I'm sick of you fucking feminist asshats.

 Death to Brianna @chatterwhiteman 9m
@spacekatgal I'm going to rape your filthy ass until you bleed, then choke you to death with your husband's tiny Asian penis

 Death to Brianna @chatterwhiteman 10m
@spacekatgal I've got a K-Bar and I'm coming to your house so I can shove it up your ugly feminist cunt.

 Death to Brianna @chatterwhiteman 11m
@spacekatgal Guess what bitch? I now know where you live. You and Frank live at

RETWEETS LIKES
7,756   2,716

11:57 AM - 11 Oct 2014

FIGURE 2.3

enforcement agencies (Allen, 2015b). The elderly mother of another Gamergate critic, designer Caroline Sinders, was also targeted (Sinders, 2015). In mid-to-late 2015, software developer Randi Lee Harper moved cities after a wave of harassment made it clear that her home address was well known to those threatening her:

> After all of the threats, I realized I couldn't stay in my old apartment. I was tired of wearing pants, and I always had to wear pants, because I didn't know when the police were going to show up. People were sending me threats in the mail. Who the hell sends snail mail with threats? Fucking weirdos, that's who. Hello, email, have you heard of it? I was always paranoid walking outside. I was getting messages saying people were going to come to (address where I lived) and kill me.[6]

The supposed 'leaderless' structure of Gamergate enabled members to disavow responsibility for such actions (or, not infrequently, claim that victims were orchestrating their own victimisation for attention). However, a core group of 'channers' were highly active in developing and orchestrating Gamergate strategy which included various 'operations' with the specific intention of deflecting criticism of the movement. In September 2014, as Gamergate's campaign of online abuse drew increasingly negative media attention, channers proposed the Twitter hashtag #notyourshield as part of what they called a 'special jamming op [operation]' to 'jam' or deflect accusations that Gamergate was misogynist and driven largely by reactionary white male gamers.[7] On 4chan, instructions were disseminated that gamers who were not 'white, cis and male' should post under the #notyourshield hashtag on Twitter and demand that journalists 'stop using [women and minority groups] as a shield' to deflect criticism of 'social justice warriors'. The hashtag #notyourshield was then presented on Twitter as a spontaneous grass-roots movement of women and sexually and racially diverse gamers claiming that they were being 'silenced' by critics of Gamergate. The hashtag involved a large proportion of 'sockpuppets' accounts from channers posing as women and people of colour, but it also appears to have mobilised a diverse group of gamers to express solidarity with Gamergate and gamer culture (Johnston, 2014).

One of the dangers of an ostensibly leaderless and unstructured movement is that it tends towards entropy. Tensions within Gamergate increased as gamers polarised around divergent concerns, leading to infighting (King and Cuen, 2015). Figures within the Gamergate movement began subjecting each other to the same tactics of abuse, including doxing and bomb threats, that had previously terrorised the targets of the movement (Pless, 2015). These internal conflicts and an inability to articulate a clear agenda have significantly blunted the momentum of Gamergate and further discredited it in the eyes of the mass media. Those gamers with genuine concerns about games media, and cultural and political clashes in games culture, de-affiliated from Gamergate over time and it is now reduced to a much smaller rump of support. Nonetheless, the specific targets of Gamergate such as Quinn and Sarkeesian continue to be vilified in the right wing and 'men's rights' online media and blogs that have emerged as the champion of the Gamergate cause. They've been forced to curtail their public appearances, limit their engagement with social media and engage professional security at public events to ensure their safety (Filipovic, 2015).

The subpolitics of online abuse and resistance

In many ways, the internal dynamics of Gamergate reflect the intricacy of online 'subpolitics' (Beck 1997) as users are mobilised around general points of agreement and interest in ways that give rise to collective action. Drawing on Beck's (1997) notion of the subpolitical, Lindgren and Linde (2012) identify the ways in which the micro-practices of internet users are channelled and aggregated en masse into politically salient movements that emerge outside the space of institutionalised politics. In this 'subpolitical' process, shared patterns in the personal decisions and practices of thousands or millions of users can take public form and exert political force from outside formal political structures. Like many new social movements, Gamergate has been at pains to emphasise its non-aligned and 'apolitical' orientation against its targets which it paints as 'political' and therefore 'prejudiced'. By this logic, being 'political' is synonymous with being partisan. Instead Gamergate sought to advance a 'common sense' understanding that rejects any scrutiny of power dynamics within gaming as a form of 'bias' against the white, heterosexual male majority that dominate the industry. 'Gators were bound together by shared affect and mutually agreed sources of outrage rather than a coherent agenda, as semi-articulated intuitions about gender and 'politics' gave rise to a mass movement designed to overwhelm the online spaces for women and other users to express their concerns about gaming culture.

The specifically subpolitical dimensions of Gamergate were expressed through the rearticulation of gendered and sexual difference in misogynist terms that marked women, in particular, as out of place in the gaming industry and on social media more generally. The over-writing of diversity as *perversity* was evident in the highly sexualised caricatures of Quinn and other women in the gaming industry developed and circulated by Gamergate to justify their ongoing campaign of abuse and misrepresentation. This represented a collective albeit partially coordinated project of abuse with the aim of public exclusion. As Quinn revealed when she published their chatlogs, there was a core group of 'channers' who strategically activated the concerns of 'gamers' in order to create a mass movement around their ongoing harassment of Quinn and other supposed 'social justice warriors'. This project extended beyond their own various rationalisations to connect with the long-standing public traditions of maintaining homosocial exclusivity through misogynist harassment and other forms of abuse. This tradition was embedded and indeed ritualised within the homosocial milieu of 4chan, 8chan and Reddit, where the fetishisation of anonymity acted as a cypher for homogeneity, and personal identifiers were considered unnecessary because users were presumed to be white, heterosexual and male.

The subpolitics of online abuse cannot be disentangled from site architecture and administration because these have a formative influence on the discursive norms that emerge in different online contexts. The 'toxic technocultures' exemplified by Gamergate have been fostered on 4chan and Reddit where policies against harassment and doxing are rarely enforced, enabling the formation of abusive networks who then actively exploit social media architecture 'aggregating large audiences while offering little protection from potential harassment victims' (Massanari, 2015: 5). These abusive networks shift strategically between the anonymity of the 'chan' image-boards, which protect user identity while enabling them to coordinate harassment, onto social media, whose rich field of personal and identifying information provides ample ammunition for harassment campaigns. As Phillips (2015: 25–26) observed, 'successful trolling is often dependent on the target's lack of anonymity, or at least their willingness to disclose real-life attachments, interests and vulnerabilities'.

Since online abuse is subpolitical, it is often seen as subcriminal – that is, not serious enough to warrant intervention by police. Even where online abuse is criminalised under existing laws against harassment and stalking, police rarely enforce them. Online abuse victims regularly find that police lack the relevant training and understanding to respond to online abuse (Citron, 2014). The FBI has reportedly opened a case on Gamergate but no arrests have been forthcoming at the time of writing (Jason, 2015). After meeting with the FBI, Congresswoman Katherine Clark of Massachusetts, the congresswoman of Gamergate target Brianna Wu, complained that Gamergate and online abuse 'is clearly just not one of their priorities' (quoted in Merlan, 2015). In 2015, Twitter executives identified Gamergate as a key incident in which users are 'completely overwhelmed by those who are trying to silence healthy discourse' (Gadd, 2015). Twitter has since flagged a number of changes, including an increased number of personnel in the Twitter support team that responds to complaints, and an expanded safety policy (Gadd, 2015). Reddit has also announced a policy change to prohibit harassment, stating: 'Instead of promoting free expression of ideas, we are seeing our open policies stifling free expression; people avoid participating for fear of their personal and family safety.'[8]

These have proven to be largely symbolic gestures. Outbreaks of mass harassment are a daily occurrence on social media, prompting those targeted and their allies to take matters into their own hands. American software engineer Randi Lee Harper developed the 'Good Game Auto Blocker', a third party application for users to automatically block large numbers of Twitter users associated with Gamergate. Her approach was so successful that it has since been adopted by Twitter which now allows users to share lists of 'blocked' users between them. Harper also founded the Online Abuse Prevention Initiative to support research and advocacy for victims of online abuse.[9] Zoe Quinn has founded the Crash Override Network, a pro bono support, advice and referral service for victims of large-scale online abuse.[10] Sarkeesian has been particularly outspoken about the ferocity of online abuse and its impacts, and in recognition of her work was named as one of *Time Magazine*'s 100 most influential people in 2015.[11] The advocacy of the women targeted by Gamergate has led to new calls for the criminalisation of online abuse and enforcement of existing laws against threats and abuse (Merlan, 2015).

Conclusion

Gamergate exemplifies the clash between the male-dominated and anonymous culture of online interaction that characterised Web 1.0, and a diversifying body of social media users with publicly available identities. Within gamer culture, abuse was normalised as a discursive strategy to maintain 'gamer' hegemony within the gaming industry and press. In many regards, the prevailing rhetoric of insult reflects the kinds of mutual abuse and misogyny common amongst all-male peer groups and institutions. As this conduct was challenged by diversifying cohorts of players and developers, this previously inwardly facing subculture developed an aggressively outwardly facing 'public' which used social media to engage in the abuse of its critics. The scale of the attacks against women such as Quinn and Sarkeesian reflects, Jeong (2015) argues, the deep-seated belief that 'these women don't belong on the Internet'. This belief drove the premeditated orchestration of abuse within the anonymity of the 'chan' boards and rolled out on social media. Gamergate sought a privileged, depersonalised public position for itself as the authoritative voice on gaming while characterising its opponents and victims as merely private, partial and trivial. In this process, it sought to recuperate and assert the hegemonic kinds of speech available to members of homogenous publics, ringfenced by abuse and threats against those whose diversity might threaten the status quo.

While the decentralisation of public discourse away from the mass media is a much celebrated correlate of internet technology, Gamergate raises important questions about the standards of public discourse online. Habermas's (1984) assertion that the speech act assumes good faith on behalf of the other party describes a form of intersubjective trust operative in public discourse that was actively breached and repeatedly manipulated by Gamergate. Gamergate's abusive broadcasting of personal information, the imitation of women and people of colour in 'sockpuppet' accounts, and disingenuous 'false flag' operations such as #notyourshield actively instrumentalised and misused the public sociability of social media to abusive effect. Woven into this sociability were pre-existing asymmetries of power based on inequalities of gender, sexuality and race that could be mobilised in an attempt to preserve the exclusivity of gaming and online publics more broadly. While comparable distortions are present in the mass media, the scale and intensity of the abuse that underpinned Gamergate would be simply unthinkable within the more regulated arena of television or newspaper. Indeed, mass media coverage had a decisive role in evaluating the competing claims of Gamergate and its critics, and ultimately dismissing Gamergate as a misogynist abuse campaign rather than, as gamers claimed, a movement for 'ethics in gaming journalism'.

The active resistance that Quinn, Sarkeesian and others displayed while under attack by Gamergate has earned them widespread recognition and acclaim, and appears to be leveraging cultural change within the gaming industry. On 24 September 2015, Quinn and Sarkeesian were invited to speak at the United Nations in New York as part of the launch of a UN report on 'cyber-violence' against girls and women. With other high-profile women in information technology, Quinn, Sarkeesian and Harper visited the think-tank Google Ideas to discuss the impact of online abuse and potential solutions. Their criticisms of the representation of women in video gaming appear to be shifting industry attitudes. In 2015, major gaming studios announced a raft of games with playable major female characters dressed in functional attire, rather than the second-tier, highly sexualised female characters that have predominated in video gaming (Kubas-Meyer, 2015). Meanwhile, Zoe Quinn has recently announced a contract for the publication of her autobiography and a forthcoming movie based on her experiences with Gamergate (Figure 2.4).

Nonetheless, Gamergate has promoted a culture of fear within gaming and social media more generally by illustrating the potential fate of women deemed to be too vocal or opinionated online. As game developer Elizabeth Sampat noted, 'the truth about Zoe Quinn is that every woman in the industry is one unhinged ex-partner away from being Zoe Quinn' (quoted in Allen, 2015a). This places girls and

Pinned Tweet

Zoë "Shitpost" Quinn @UnburntWitch · 7 Nov 2015

Two announcements in one:
1 - I'm publishing a book with Touchstone,
a Simon and Schuster imprint
2 - That book is being made into a movie

🔁 772   ❤ 2.4K   •••   View conversation

FIGURE 2.4

women in a double bind. For women in gaming, and indeed many other professions, social media participation is crucial to their professional reputations and career progression. However, their personal characteristics and attributes as women continue to be stigmatised within the misogynist variants of internet culture and thus they are vulnerable to ostracism and humiliation where those attributes are abusively foregrounded. '[D]isclosing information about the self is necessary in order to reap the benefits from these technological tools' (Ellison et al., 2011: 20), and yet it is precisely that personal information that can be incorporated into their abuse. In Gamergate, those 'gamers' who sought to preserve the internet and gaming as exclusively male took advantage of anonymous fora to de-identify themselves while they actively attacked women on social media using the personal information they found online.

The intensity of emotion evident in Gamergate suggests that more was at stake than just protecting gamers' preferred genres of video games and gaming press. As the Frankfurt School theorists argued, feelings of alienation and anxiety are actively channelled by cultural industries into revenge fantasies and spectacles of power that evade consumers in their everyday lives. In this process, legitimately political problems that generate experiences of dislocation and uncertainty are obscured within faux-conflicts. Faced with experiences of dislocation and uncertainty, many boys and men have turned to computers and new technology as an alternative foundation for masculine identity and accomplishment (Kendall, 2000). Gamergate's desperate attempts to exclude and drive women and diverse users from gaming and social media can be understood as an attempt to preserve the techno-masculinity that many boys and men have invested in as a method for resolving internal anxiety and ambiguity. Social media, with its proliferation of female and diverse users, represents a direct threat to this gendered technological order and hence continues to serve as a major site in which gendered abuses and struggles for power persist.

Meanwhile, social media offers very limited protections for those particularly vulnerable to the abuse that arises in the policing of the public domain. For example, Twitter mechanics do not enable bystanders to intervene decisively when they see abuse unfolding, nor can targeted users protect themselves by, for instance, disabling notifications on a tweet that is being flooded with abuse and insults. Gamergate was in train for over six months before Twitter announced substantive changes to their service in order to protect victims, and the abuse of women such as Quinn and Sarkeesian had been ongoing at that point for even longer. It was only once international media attention had made the threat of online abuse a major public relations problem for Twitter that it began formulating a substantive response. On a commodified platform like social media, provocative or shocking content garners attention and drives traffic in a manner that other forms of content do not. This creates a context in which users have a range of incentives to generate and circulate harmful or abusive content to enhance their status online, and it is not in the immediate interest of social media sites to intervene, except to protect their reputation and avoid public backlash. The next chapter examines this logic in more detail and highlights the role of online abuse in building user profiles and profit for social media companies.

Notes

1 The chapter uses the term 'gamer' to refer specifically to those who adopt video gaming as an identity and lifestyle. People who play games without investing them with a particularly high level of emotional attachment or collective identity will be referred to as 'players'.
2 See https://twitter.com/eron_gj/status/504734708828499968.
3 www.reddit.com/r/Drama/comments/2ekx0e/im_zoe_quinns_ex_ama.
4 http://ohdeargodbees.tumblr.com/post/95188657119/once-again-i-will-not-negotiate-with-terrorists.

5 'Social justice warrior' is a pejorative term that is widely used in conservative and right wing circles to refer to people deemed to be advancing a progressive political agenda.
6 Harper described her decision to move on her blog at https://blog.randi.io/2015/09/07/quick-updates.
7 For a screenshot, see http://img.pixady.com/2014/09/202517_bwm9q3cia axi4t.jpg.
8 www.redditblog.com/2015/05/promote-ideas-protect-people.html.
9 http://onlineabuseprevention.org.
10 www.crashoverridenetwork.com.
11 http://time.com/3822727/anita-sarkeesian-2015-time-100.

Suggested links

Play Zoe Quinn's (Twitter: @UnburntWitch) award winning game Depression Quest at www.depressionquest.com.

You can access Anita Sarkeesian's (Twitter: @FemFreq) video critiques of the depictions of women in video games at her site Feminist Frequency: http://feministfrequency.com.

Randi Lee Harper (Twitter: @randileeharper) described her decision to develop an open source anti-harassment tool in a video available at https://blog.randi.io/2015/06/27/bsdcan-2015-fighting-harassment-with-open-source-tools.

Key anti-harassment organisations include Online Abuse Prevention Initiative: http://onlineabuseprevention.org and the Crash Override Network http://www.crashoverridenetwork.com.

3

BECOMING FACEBOOK FAMOUS

Commodification and exploitation on social media

Prior to the advent of social media, online abuse was often explained according to the apparently disinhibiting nature of online interaction. Of particular concern has been the anonymity or 'pseudonymity' of online interaction, where the 'gender, race, age and physical appearances of others is not immediately evident' and nor are the reactions of those interacted with (Ellison, 2001: 143). Certainly, as the last chapter suggests, the anonymity of users can inform a culture of transgression and impunity in which abuse can flourish. In contrast, many social media platforms encourage or require users to register under their legal name and provide other identifying information. However, the trend towards identifiability on social media has not proven particularly inhibiting. While pseudonymous, fake or 'sockpuppet' accounts are common in online abuse, users frequently engage in the abuse of others under their own name and identity. In fact, some users seek to publicise their abusive conduct as much as possible to a larger social media audience. The same publicity that is turned against the victim, whose personal characteristics are impugned and whose privacy is invaded, is maximised to the benefit of the perpetrator for whom the abuse acts as a kind of public and interactive performance.

This chapter asks why some users on social media publicly engage in online abuse and threats. Drawing in part on the experiences of young people gathered in focus groups, the chapter argues that the engineered sociability of social media encourages an objectifying view of the self and others that frequently manifests in the form of online abuse. The wellness of fit between online abuse and social media is encapsulated in the 'abusive idol': the online 'micro-celebrity' (Senft, 2008) who generates infamy by creating participatory, collaborative spectacles of humiliation. The term 'idol' is borrowed here from Lowenthal (1961) who observed that the types of individuals idolised by the media shift in accordance with changes in production and consumption. In an era of 'prosumption', in which economic and social capital is produced and consumed simultaneously (Ritzer and Jurgenson, 2010), social media provides a platform for abusive 'idols' who accumulate online influence by providing opportunities for the collective derogation of others. The experiences of young people emphasise how abuse and harassment is a regular occurrence within interpersonal and peer contexts, albeit one that can now be amplified by social media. However, this amplification is made possible by the commodifying logics of social media that constitute abuse as a viable strategy through which users can increase their profile and status. The chapter closes by examining how the phenomenon of 'abusive idols' illustrates the logic of abuse as a social media strategy.

Value, exchange and self-branding on social media

For many users, social media offers an unparalleled opportunity to be seen and recognised. On platforms like Twitter and Facebook, users can build a geographically unbounded network of connections to share photos, opinions and thoughts with. In turn, this content attracts visual signs of appreciation through an accumulation of 'likes', 'shares' and other quantified ratings. It doesn't take long for users to notice that some users and content attract more attention than others. Being ignored on social media signals a type of 'social death' (Lyon and Bauman, 2013) and regular social media users quickly learn the informal rules that determines the kinds of content that attracts interest. This is not dissimilar to the process of a corporation that increases the production of a popular product while discontinuing an unpopular one. On social media, this process is 'outsourced' to content providers – that is, users – to decide on the most appropriate strategy to garner attention and 'ratings'. The visibility of metrics such as 'likes', 'friends' and so forth provides an immediate feedback mechanism whereby the ranking of users and their content is provided to them (and typically displayed to others) in real time, encouraging them to adjust their self-presentation and content production to maximise their exposure. These systems of ranking and ordering are not only the implicit backdrop to social media sociability, but they directly inform social media algorithms that prioritise popular users and content by, for example, featuring them more prominently within automatically curated news streams (Van Dijck, 2013: 130). In this process, social and economic forms of exchange become indistinct, as the economic incentives of social media platforms to drive traffic are reworked into an inducement to users to raise their profile.

The quantification of popularity and attention on social media produces a pervasive milieu of objectification. In order to set up a user profile and engage on social media, users are usually encouraged to provide a picture of themselves, supply a name and other information such as their profession or hobbies, and then generate content that purportedly reflects their personal opinions, sentiments and experiences. In this process, users take an audit of their most and least marketable characteristics, and seek to present themselves online in the most favourable light. This ethos of objectifying assessment and competitive ranking dates back to the formative period of social media. Somewhat infamously, the predecessor to Facebook was Facemash, a site launched in 2003 for Harvard students to rate and compare the attractiveness of female students. Facemash mimicked other popular 'ratings' sites such as RateMyFace and HotOrNot, where viewers could scroll through images of people, and compare and rate their attractiveness. In this process, people become interchangeable objects, evacuated of subjectivity and reduced to simple categories and quantifiable differences. A key difference between Facebook and Facemash is that, on Facemash, women were ranked and compared without their consent, whereas on Facebook, people are invited to actively shape the basis on which they are publicly assessed and compared.

For casual social media users, inducements towards self-objectification in the service of increased visibility and exposure may be ineffective or ignored entirely. Users who, for example, primarily use Facebook to communicate with relatives and friends overseas, or who enjoy a curated news stream on Twitter, may be unconcerned with the number of 'friends' or 'likes' they accumulate. However, 'opting out' of this competitive system is becoming increasingly untenable for many young people and professionals. Personal image construction has been actively championed as a way of securing control and employment within an unstable or, in neoliberal terms, 'flexible' labour market (Hearn, 2010: 205). Social media activity is increasingly understood as part of a 'self-brand' that individuals should develop in order to increase their social and economic opportunities (Banet-Weiser, 2012: 55). In a time where transitions from youth to adulthood, and between career pathways, are increasingly uncertain, the self-brand offers a 'detachable, saleable image or narrative' (Hearn, 2010: 198) that aims to facilitate mobility across multiple spheres of life. This self-brand is built up in many contexts, however social media participation constitutes a particularly visible and publicly accessible manifestation of the self-brand. As such, social media is integrated into consumerist practices of self-presentation and self-construction that are closely linked to ideologies of personal/economic growth.

Young people can find that they are expected to construct, maintain and promote their social media profile to others. In one focus group, Alicia noted that 'friending' or following her employer's corporate page on Facebook was a precondition of her casual employment. Arguably, this places an implicit pressure on Alicia to interact with her employer's Facebook posts, which in turn would increase the prominence of her employer's posts in the news feeds of Alicia's Facebook network and provide free publicity for the company. Since 'friending' is a reciprocal arrangement on Facebook, this necessarily gave her employer access to her personal Facebook profile, which could have ramifications for her employment if she was, for example, to post about a negative work experience. Rather than risk 'repercussions', she felt tacitly obliged to censor her Facebook use to the point of abandoning her page altogether. She said:

I think you have to be really careful thinking about who's viewing your page. For example, I had to become a friend with my work on Facebook, and now I just don't post anything at all really because I have to think about it really carefully, about if I post anything they're going to see it and could have possible repercussions. So I think you have to think really carefully about who's seeing it now because a lot of people don't know who's viewing their page through friends of friends or whatever, so you have to be careful about what you put out there.

Social media is promoted to users as an important utility spanning their social and professional lives. As Alicia's quote indicates, this permeability between different spheres of life can catalyse, in effect, the colonisation of the social by the professional, particularly amongst those users concerned with their employability and job prospects. Companies routinely screen and reject potential employees based on their social media and online activities, while the job security of existing employees can be placed at risk over online transgressions (Citron, 2014: 8). Those social media users that fail to present a consistently reputable 'self-brand' online are at risk of being labelled morally derelict, endangering their employment and poisoning their future prospects. Alan recalled:

One of my best mates back at home, he had his first job interview after he graduated uni, and at the job interview, they brought him in and said, like, 'Sign into your Facebook and Twitter accounts right now or you can leave'.

Some young people responded to social media surveillance with practices designed to disrupt linkages between their personal life and their 'public' face on social media. For example, Trudy made her Facebook profile 'public' (that is, available to all) but did not post 'status updates', instead using the Facebook 'Messenger' function to keep all personal communication private.[1] She had strict rules about the kinds of photos that friends and others could post about her to the site and avoided circumstances in which inappropriate photos might be taken.

TRUDY: I have my Facebook on public, I really don't care, because I don't post statuses, like everything's through messages and events [the Facebook 'events' function enables people to organise events such as parties] anyway.

LOUIS: What about photos?

TRUDY: They're just photos, there's some ugly ones, but like I'm not going to let someone take a photo of me that's later going to compromise a job or anything like that.

In this focus group, Sam referred to Trudy's strategy as being 'completely public' and counter-posed this approach to friends who did the 'total opposite' and created Facebook accounts using fake names (in breach of Facebook's terms of service). Other young people described friends who altered their names, genders, ages and other information on Facebook in an effort to maintain a distinction between their 'personal' and 'public' selves. As one participant suggested, it was a way of becoming 'un-Google-able' in order to mitigate the reputational risks of social media. To a certain degree, both strategies – a carefully managed 'public' profile or a 'fake' profile – reflected small subversions of the omnipresence of social media, but they were not necessarily discontinuous with the calculated manufacturing of a 'self-brand'. Setting her Facebook account to 'public' enabled Trudy to display herself to possible employers and others in a manner that appears guileless and open but in fact required constant self-regulation. The alternate approach described by Sam involved the creation of an alternative online persona that, by virtue of being 'fake', promises genuine and spontaneous self-expression. This can also be reduced to another online posture or style as a way of setting the individual apart from others.

In short, it is difficult to escape entirely the commodifying and objectifying logic of social media platforms. As Banet-Weiser (2012: 57) notes, even if we don't set out to build a brand, 'the logic of online sites and the presence of feedback means that one's online presence will be viewed by others using the same rubric to judge brands: through evaluation, ranking, and judgement, and with the ideal of visibility in mind'. Even attempted subversions can be recuperated as a style or strategy that builds a user's self-brand by imbuing it with valuable characteristics and inflections. However, self-brands are not endlessly elastic. They need to be viewed by others as a more-or-less accurate representation of the user. This limits the extent to which users can seek advantage within social media's competitive ranking systems. As Dobson (2015: 10) observes, social media profiles are generally assumed to 'proceed from a premise of agentic, conscious, and "authentic" self-authorship'. Profiles that are understood to have been manipulated for the purpose of self-promotion breach this assumption and attract pejorative attributions. In focus groups, social media users who were seen to be openly pursuing large numbers of 'friends', 'likes' and other rankings were reviled as 'fakes' and 'attention seekers'. Young people were at pains to emphasise their modest ambitions for their social media use, in which their photos and online content were understood to be continuous with 'who they were' more generally.

While young people in focus groups often affected a disinterest in their social media network, it was clearly that many had actively worked to expand far beyond their existing interpersonal connections with families and friends. A few dozen 'friends' on Facebook, or a few desultory 'likes' on a photo, was simply embarrassing, and young people often spoke of having hundreds or even thousands of 'friends' on Facebook and other platforms. Once a critical mass of 'ratings' had been accumulated on a social media platform, users were hesitant to expand much further. The requirement that a 'self-brand' appears 'authentic' introduces the contradictory obligation to deny that any process of self-promotion is underway on social media, even to the user that is engaged in it, and it also generated an unclear cut-off point beyond which users were reluctant (or did not need) to pursue further 'ratings'. Being seen to seek more 'friends' and so forth, at a level beyond others in the same peer group, exposed users to allegations of 'attention seeking' and 'desperation'.

From self-branding to self-exploitation

As discussed, the 'authenticity' requirement necessarily limits the extent to which users can accumulate 'ratings' while still maintaining the appearance that their 'self-brand' reflects who they 'really' are.

However, this requirement is not a compulsory feature of a self-brand. The appearance of authenticity can be dispensed with by users in the interests of garnering online attention and positioning themselves more advantageously within the hierarchy of social media. Social media users with the specific aim of expanding their online networks and profile can engage in a self-conscious process of self-exploitation in order to accomplish wider social media exposure. In self-exploitation, the logic of self-objectification is fully embraced by the user and taken to its natural conclusion so that 'the very stuff of lived experience', such as bodies and personal experiences, are exchanged 'in the service of promotion and possible profit' (Hearn, 2010: 213). The term 'self-exploitation' has at times been applied as a pejorative descriptor of the self-manufacture of sexual or nude digital images, particularly by minors (Karaian, 2015). In this section, the term is used to refer more broadly to a conscious process of self-objectification undertaken by social media users in the pursuit of greater exposure and 'rankings'.

Self-exploitation can be a highly successful albeit risky social media strategy. For example, in August 2015, Christian vloggers and married couple Sam and Nia Rader garnered worldwide attention when they uploaded a video to YouTube entitled 'HUSBAND SHOCKS WIFE WITH PREGNANCY ANNOUNCEMENT'. The video depicted Sam stealing a sample of his wife's urine from an unflushed toilet and then 'surprising' her with a positive pregnancy test. The video quickly accumulated millions of views and was widely covered in the mass media (Jones, 2015a) but the social media response to the Raders was mixed. While many comments on YouTube and Twitter expressed excitement for the couple, others questioned their motives for recording and publicising such a personal moment. This was exacerbated by the Raders' activity on Twitter and YouTube. Subsequent videos and 'tweets' suggested they were closely tracking their social media metrics. In an interview with Buzzfeed, Sam Rader was clear that he recorded the initial pregnancy video 'definitely hoping' it would go 'viral', adding 'I've always had a dream to be famous' (McNeal and Zarrell, 2015). He closely tracked the number of views that the video attracted, sending out this tweet within 24 hours:

Sam&Nia
@SamAndNia

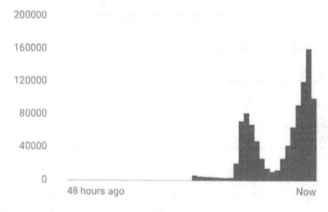

Wow guys! One million views in 24 hours!!

RETWEETS LIKES
20 147

2 27 AM - 7 Aug 2015

FIGURE 3.1

Three days after the 'pregnancy announcement' video, the Raders uploaded another video called 'Our Baby Had a Heartbeat'. On camera, the highly emotional couple disclosed that Nia had miscarried. Shortly afterwards, they gave a range of media interviews, and tweeted about the number of views and followers their 'tiny baby' had garnered them (Figure 3.2).

After an initial flurry of sympathy, the scepticism that had been gathering online since the announcement of Nia's pregnancy reached a crescendo. There was general speculation by vloggers and YouTube commenters that the couple had faked both the pregnancy and the miscarriage (Figures 3.3–3.5).

A subsequent video released by the Raders provided an ambiguous response to their critics. In the video, Sam stated that Nia's pregnancy

 **Sam&Nia**
@SamAndNia

 ⚙ 👤 Follow

Our tiny baby brought 10M views to her video &
100k new people into our lives. She turned our
life around & brought us closer together.

RETWEETS	LIKES	
85	520	

5:25 AM - 10 Aug 2015

↩ ♺ ♥ •••

FIGURE 3.2

 **Cloaked Figure**
@ACloakedFigure

⚙ 👤 Follow

Who are these Sam and Nia people?
Pregnancy announcement gets 10 million
views in 4 days and now a miscarriage video?
Hmmm

2:06 AM - 11 Aug 2015

↩ ♺ ♥ •••

FIGURE 3.3

 **AJ**
@jenoradio

⚙ 👤 Follow

Unpopular opinion of the day: I don't believe
Sam and Nia's pregnancy/miscarriage vlog. I
smell a reality show shopper. The next
Duggars? 😳

LIKES	
2	

7:29 AM - 11 Aug 2015

↩ ♺ ♥ •••

FIGURE 3.4

Sarah
@redfairSarah

Sam Rader hope this miscarriage news is not some publicity stunt #Nia

12:20 PM - 11 Aug 2015

FIGURE 3.5

and miscarriage 'wasn't fake' but instead it 'was staged' by God, and it's not their fault that 'the world is choosing to be deceived' (Jones, 2015b). Regardless of the facts, the Rader's conduct clearly demonstrates the role of self-exploitation in building a social media brand and its potential risks. The initial pregnancy video launched them into viral stardom, and their YouTube channel currently has 400,000 subscribers who they keep entertained with revealing videos about family life. In this process, the couple's children, extended family and intimate life have been incorporated into semi-scripted performances designed to appeal to a wide audience. The manner in which the couple attained their online celebrity, and their willingness to commodify their private lives in this way, continues to draw widespread suspicion and criticism. Nonetheless, focusing solely on the motives and morality of social media users who engage in self-exploitation overlooks their often constrained economic and social position. Writing about the Raders, Hess (2015b) suggested 'this is about more than just the hits. It's about the money.' Vloggers can generate (a usually very modest) income through YouTube advertising services (and other methods including paid content and product placement) and it's likely that this income would be very welcome for the Naders. Hess (2015b) writes:

> Because ads aren't served on every video view, and because You-Tube collects 45 percent of a channel's ad revenue, vloggers stand to make just a few thousand dollars [$US] for every million views they rack up. Still, for a small-town vlogging family subsisting on one nurse's salary like the Raders are, a video viewed 12 million times is a hefty unexpected windfall. It's hard to begrudge them

that. After months of videos topping out at 20,000 views – ones largely created by stay-at-home mom Nia, caring for two kids while filming her every move – it's likely the family could really use the money.

Marwick and boyd (2011: 140) argue that celebrity has become a set of strategies and practices that place 'fame' on a continuum that is at least potentially available to the everyday social media user. Importantly, movement up this continuum is not equally available to all users. Self-exploitation is driven to a large degree by the relative scarcity of resources and opportunities that everyday social media users have to hand, and this includes their limited options to create content that might attract attention, and thus views, clicks, 'likes' and other measures of social media success. The publication of intimate moments and personal details is often the most readily available way to accomplish this. The revealing of the body, in particular, is likely to trigger interest in ways that other forms of personal disclosure do not. This can include sexualised and erotic imagery, as discussed in the next chapter, but eroticism is only one variant of explicitness. Sam Nader's use of an unflushed toilet in the couple's pregnancy video hints at the capacity of bodily waste to simultaneously fascinate and repel. Focus group discussions identified a range of other examples in which the bodily fluids were expelled in the service of self-exploitation.

Particularly prominent in focus group discussions were videos circulating on social media in which young people record themselves engaging in often vulgar or humiliating stunts to induce other users to share, like and comment on the video. The 'condom challenge', for example, involves YouTube videos of teenagers and young people snorting unrolled condoms up one nostril and pulling it from the other nostril or their mouth. These videos attract mostly disgusted comments from viewers while accumulating hundreds of thousands of views. Other 'gross-out' videos involve the ingestion of foul substances typically followed by their bodily expulsion.

TIM: There's those [YouTube] channels where they do the 'cinnamon challenge' and the 'milk challenge' and things like that and people like it.

FACILITATOR: Okay, so what's a cinnamon challenge?

SEBASTIAN: You have to eat a spoonful of cinnamon without dying. And like the milk challenge, they drink a litre of milk without spewing.

JUSTINE: Yeah cos if you drink a litre of milk, you just vomit…

SEBASTIAN: And they colour it and stuff so you throw up like red vomit.

MIRIAM: Yeah, colour vomit.

FACILITATOR: Okay, so if you wanted to get a whole bunch of Facebook friends or likes or something, you could if you wanted…

STEPHEN: Do stupid stuff, yeah pretty much.

FACILITATOR [INCREDULOUS]: That's an option that's just available.

TIM: Yeah.

HUAN: Yeah.

FACILITATOR: And if you happen to throw up the best pink coloured milk presumably…

HUAN: It's like a quick rise to fame kind of thing.

SEBASTIAN: Yeah, I know this band and they did that for the music video. So when the guy yelled, it was just him throwing up milk.

The music video described by Sebastian, in which the musicians vomit coloured milk, ultimately proved to be a successful way for the band to garner more views and thus publicity for their band (see Styles, 2012). The use of 'gross-out' videos for a 'quick rise to fame' was so common that some young people complained it was inhibiting their enjoyment of social media altogether.

ASHLEY: I don't even look at Facebook news feed because it's all that [gross-out videos] now.

LANA: If I was to have my Facebook open right now, there would be something like that.

ISABELLA: And it's just because people have liked it, and then it just like throws onto everyone else's.

ASHLEY: Or even if they watched it.

LANA: Yeah, it turns up.

ASHLEY: If they comment, like 'You're disgusting' or something, it'll still [appear on my news feed]… And you're just forced to look at it while you scroll past.

'Gross-out' videos put young people's bodies to work in a provocative and transgressive fashion in exchange for the cultural capital that accrues to the producers of 'viral' content. As the discussion above indicates, social media users who interact with these videos on Facebook in order to register their disgust 'throw' the video onto their friend's timelines; that is, they are perpetuating the 'virality' or spread of the video by engaging with it, which according to Facebook's underlying software architecture signals that the video should then be displayed to the 'friends' of the user. This process increases the exposure of the video exponentially, earning the 'star' of the video significant numbers of followers, likes, comments and other measures of popularity.

Like other forms of self-exploitation, this strategy can exact a high toll upon young people. In the following discussion, participants described 'Tampon Girl', a viral video from 2012 in which a teenager appears to remove a tampon from her body and suck the menstrual fluid from it.

ISABELLA: Like to get Facebook famous, that's the craze now.

SARAH: Yeah, people just make videos to become Facebook famous.

REECE: I don't know if it's the same thing you're talking about, but a few months ago there was a girl and she ate a tampon, and it had hundreds of thousands of likes…

ISABELLA: What was the point?

REECE: I haven't seen it but…

LANA: She just wanted attention.

JAYLEE: And then she got all this attention and in the end she was like 'it was fake, you guys are so stupid'.

LANA: But it wasn't fake.

JAYLEE: Yeah, she went on for so long saying how real it was.

ISABELLA: And these girls post these videos or whatever and then they'll say, 'I don't care, it's my body I can do what I want with it. No one hate this video.'

LANA: Yeah 'don't hate', yeah.

The 'Tampon Girl' video has been viewed millions of times and generated hundreds of thousands of social media followers for its young 'star'. Reportedly, she also received a torrent of death threats and encouragement to kill herself (Hoffman, 2013). In a subsequent 'confession video' uploaded to YouTube, 'Tampon Girl' describes her regret for circulating the video, and the impact of the subsequent abuse and harassment on her reputation and wellbeing. She describes being removed from school and hospitalised once the video went 'viral'. Even her apology attracted further abuse, with YouTube comments such as:

Seriously sterilize this thing before it lays eggs.

your a sad dumb bitch who is so lonely and deprived that you do anything for attention. your horrible. so damn fat i see why you would eat a bloody tampon

Bitch, you mother fucking vampire bitch face cunt bitch fuck

The 'Tampon Girl' video suggests that some young people's attempts to gain online notoriety can take very concerning forms. The maintenance of a perceived link between online self-display and a 'true self' is fundamental to the value of the user's 'self-brand'. In the search for increased social media status and reach, some users may compromise or sever this link as they engage in forms of self-exploitation, such as stunts and vulgar displays, that symbolise an overt capitulation to the quantified logics of social media virality. The highly qualified appeal of self-exploitation is that it takes the primary commodity of social media – the personal data and characteristics of users – and puts it to work for users, albeit within the pre-determined hierarchy of social media. While this strategy may accumulate significant online 'ratings' it can damage the integrity of the user's self-brand with ramifications beyond their reputation on social media. 'Tampon Girl', the Raders and the various 'stars' of 'gross-out' videos must now contend with the after-effects of online displays that have attracted a range of pejorative attributions from revulsion and disgust to accusations of mental illness and narcissism.

Idols of abuse and the logic of online abuse

An alternative and arguably less risky strategy to self-exploitation is the exploitation of others. This removes the user from the cycle of objectification and humiliation evident in self-exploitation, such that the value generated by exploitation accrues to the user but its harms do not. Instead, the harms of exploitation are borne by the person/s targeted by this strategy. Repudiating or humiliating other social media users can constitute a highly salient form of content generation that, in and of itself, invites attention and interaction from other users. A small 'cottage industry' of responses to the Raders and the Tampon Girl video has emerged on YouTube and other social media sites analysing the minutiae of their behaviour and speculating on their motivations and character. This invites interaction and feedback from other social media users also keen to express their derision. This form of content production is 'prosumptive' (Ritzer and Jurgenson, 2010) in the sense that it is produced even as it is consumed in a kind of rolling collaborative spectacle, in which the circulation of emotionally compelling, spontaneous, revealing content produces value for both the platform (in the form of increased traffic and therefore advertising revenue) and for the user (in the form of increased exposure and 'ratings').

The 'prosumption' of online abuse can become so integral to the self-brands of some users that it signals a new permutation of online public personae. Lowenthal (1961) observed a major shift in media coverage in the twentieth century from an early focus on 'idols of production' – that is, people in business and politics engaged in the productive sphere – to 'idols of consumption' as the mass media reorientated around the personal lives of celebrities and sports stars. He argued that mass media 'hero-selection' no longer reflected social and economic realities and instead consumers spend their leisure time reading 'almost exclusively about the people who are directly, or indirectly, providing for the reader's leisure time' (Lowenthal, 1961: 116). In a similar vein, it might be said that social media enables and rewards 'idols of abuse' who actively facilitate and orchestrate mass campaigns of online abuse for the enjoyment of their followers. Abuse becomes a commodity as interpersonal harassment and threat is imbued with additional value, including the promise of peer recognition and acclaim, reflected in the accumulation of online ratings and the potential translation of online social capital into broader cultural and economic capital.

A key example is the American Hunter Moore, who in 2010 created the website *Is Anyone Up* that enabled users to upload nude images of other people, often linked to their social media profiles on Facebook and Twitter. In order to protect himself from potential law suits,

Moore created a submission form in which other users uploaded images and information to the site, which under United States law (specifically section 230 of the Communication Decency Act of 1996) minimised his liability for the content submitted by others. The site brought the issue of 'revenge porn' to international attention as thousands of women and men found that their nude and private images were being hosted on the site without their consent, often alongside identifying information and malicious commentary. The circulation of these images was deeply humiliating to victims and enabled sustained campaigns of harassment. Victims could find themselves targeted on social media, at home and work through threatening emails and phone calls. Moore typically responded to victim complaints or legal threats by reposting their private image and triggering a new wave of vilification.

Moore's disregard for those victimised by his site, and his facilitation of campaigns of online abuse, was key to his appeal. Despite mass media condemnation, the site came to attract almost a quarter of a million unique visitors per day, earning Moore a significant amount of money from advertising revenue on the site (Dodero, 2012). The most ardent of Moore's Twitter fans called themselves #TheFamily and collectively tweeted hundreds of thousands or even millions of times a day. They actively participated in the harassment of Moore's detractors, such as victim advocate Charlotte Laws, who had pressed for the police investigation into Moore after her daughter's images were published on his site. Once Moore became aware of Law's identity, she found herself the target of a campaign of abuse and terrorisation including threats of death and rape via telephone and email (Laws, 2013).

Laws was able to uncover compelling evidence that a significant proportion of images hosted on *Is Anyone Up?* had been unlawfully hacked from private online accounts (Laws, 2013). She passed this information to the FBI, and Moore closed the site in 2012 as police began investigating victim complaints. During this time, Moore was able to parlay his abusive 'self-brand' into income through related activities including DJing and party hosting. In January 2014, Moore and another man, Charles Evens, were arrested on multiple charges including conspiracy, computer hacking and aggravated identity theft (AP, 2014). Prosecutors contended that Evens had been engaged by Moore to hack into online accounts and sell him nude and private images. In

February 2015, Moore pleaded guilty to unauthorized access to a computer, aiding and abetting unauthorized access of a computer, and identity theft (Kreps, 2015). He was sentenced to 30 months in prison and a US$2,000 fine.

Moore's conviction has been widely championed in the mass media and online as a just outcome for victims. For his hundreds of thousands of social media users, Moore was a fallen hero. After the closure of his site, Moore's Twitter following increased from 50,000 to 580,000 until Twitter eventually shut down his account. Even to this day, members of The Family still mournfully tweet about the loss of the 'The Father' and hurriedly join Twitter accounts claiming to be Hunter Moore in their thousands, before drifting off once the account is revealed to be fake. The production and consumption of abusive content was integral to the 'self-branding' strategies not only of Moore himself, but for hundreds of thousands of admirers and followers who sought to participate in the abuse as part of their own online self-identities. His notoriety spawned a number of imitators, including revenge porn sites that attempted to blackmail victims into paying hundreds of dollars for the removal of images (Salter and Crofts, 2015).

Gamergate, discussed in the previous chapter, also produced its own 'abusive idols'. A number of vloggers attempted to capitalise upon the fury directed at Quinn and Sarkeesian, creating short YouTube videos disparaging the two women. This significantly raised their online profile, enabling them to generate YouTube advertising revenue and by soliciting donations via crowdfunding accounts such as Patreon (Allen, 2015a). They now enjoy quasi-celebrity status in the right wing corners of social media and online news. Perhaps one of the main beneficiaries of the Gamergate saga is the British journalist Milo Yiannopoulos whose media career was substantively revived by his vocal support for Gamergate and his disparagement of Gamergate targets. In a series of articles for right wing website Breitbart, Yiannopoulos gave credence to various Gamergate-sourced allegations about Zoe Quinn and Anita Sarkeesian, whom he described as 'lying, greedy, promiscuous feminist bullies' (Yiannopoloulos, 2014). This earned Yiannopoulos the loyalty of many 'gaters, whose support he has parlayed into a substantive social media following.

Yiannopoulos's prominent online status is maintained by his pejorative commentary on so-called 'social justice warriors', particularly feminists and blacks rights activists. Key to Yiannopoulos's appeal is his capacity to identify new opportunities for online abuse and harassment as he panders to the right wing tendencies of his social media following, naming activists who are subsequently targeted *en masse* by his followers. When Yianno-poulos criticised feminist writer Holly Wood, she was subject to a range of explicit online threats of rape and death on Twitter. After she tweeted at Yiannopoulos to tell his followers to stop harassing her, specifically in relation to an image she had been sent of a woman apparently being raped, he responded 'You deserve to be harassed you social justice loser' (Edwards, 2015). Some of Yiannopoulos's targets are well-connected women within the technology industry and media, and they have had some degree of success in encouraging Twitter to enforce its terms of service against harassment. In early 2016, Twitter withdrew Yiannopoulos's coveted 'verified' status on the platform (a small blue tick symbolising a 'high value' user) apparently in response to his treatment of Holly Wood. Shortly after, Yiannopoulos used Twitter to dox Gamergate target Briannu Wu, and was locked out of his account by Twitter. These sanctions are noteworthy because 'abusive idols' on social media typically enjoy impunity even where their actions are in clear breach of platform policy.

However Yiannopoloulos's repeated violations of Twitter's terms of service had become a public relations nightmare for the site. He was permanently banned from Twitter in July 2016 due to his significant role in the intense online abuse directed at Ghostbusters star and Saturday Night Live comedian Leslie Jones.

Conclusion

The phenomena of the 'abusive idol' and collectively orchestrated online harassment can be understood in terms of the inducement and shaping of collective affect within the architecture and interface of social media. Online abuse exemplifies the alienating and cruel dimensions of a 'technological rationality' (Marcuse, 1941) in which imperatives towards accumulation, competition and status instantiated within socio-technical arrangements shape social life and communication. For Marcuse (1964: 218), in technologically rationalised environments, subjects experience one another within a 'world of instrumentalities' and equivalences. On a platform in which status is measured in quantitative rather than substantive or qualitative terms, the moral distinction between abusive and non-abusive users is flattened out within totalising metrics of popularity. They are all equivalent within social media platforms orientated towards the expansion of both social and economic capital. 'Rankings' systems in social media tend to reward shocking and provocative content, whether this content involves self-exploitation or the exploitation of others. On a platform that is built on the commodification of personal information, it is quite functional for users to exploit other people rather than themselves, given that self-exploitation can expose the user to abuse and humiliation and endanger the authenticity of their self-brand. The technical architecture of social media platforms is what enables online abuse to take place, and it does this not only through technical means, but by its correspondence with a particular kind of worldview. Technological systems structured according to commodifying and alienating logics reveal and reinforce specific forms of masculine aggression and competition (Garlick, 2013). The next two chapters examine in more detail the gendered dimensions of online abuse and its correspondence within entrenched patterns of female humiliation in the reproduction of male dominance.

Note

1 Facebook Messenger acts like a private chatroom between two or more users. Unlike Facebook 'posts', which are public, content sent on the Messenger function can only be read by those invited into the conversation.

Suggested links

You can read more about the 'milk challenge' and 'cinnamon challenge' on their respective Wikipedia pages:
https://en.wikipedia.org/wiki/Milk_chugging;
https://en.wikipedia.org/wiki/Cinnamon_challenge.

Read about Charlotte Laws's (Twitter: @CharlotteLaws) efforts to expose Hunter Moore and protect women from revenge porn at:
http://jezebel.com/one-womans-dangerous-war-against-the-most-hated-man-on-1469240835.

End Revenge Porn (www.endrevengeporn.org) is a US-based campaign that supports people whose private images have been distributed without their consent and campaign for law reform.

4

ATTENTION WHORES AND GYM SELFIES

Sex and nudity in the online visual economy

Almost 40 years ago, Susan Sontag (1977: 4) observed that photos have a powerful social role in fixing the people depicted in them to particular 'truths'. By appearing as 'miniatures of reality', photos can obscure the social and cultural processes by which that meaning is attributed. The result is that the dominant interpretation of the image is frequently misunderstood as a fact captured by the image. As such, photos can act as particularly dense loci of power relations since they appear to offer *prima faci* confirmation of hegemonic norms and values, while in fact it is precisely those norms and values that shape how images are constructed, framed, circulated, displayed and understood. Once an image of a person is inserted into this circular relation, they can be reduced to 'objects that can be symbolically possessed' (Sontag, 1977: 14) and the target of 'deduction, speculation and fantasy' (p. 23).

The power of the image is particularly apparent in the age of social media, when social and intimate life is pervaded by the convergence of camera and internet technologies on smartphones, tablets and computers. Self-produced photos and video now emanate at a rapid pace from the sites of everyday life and in this process they condense and transmit the complex of relations and norms that shape not only the manufacture of the image but how it is circulated and received. On social media, these self-produced photos and videos intersect with a highly visual culture that endorses revealing forms of self-representation. This was examined in the last chapter, where the pursuit of online 'rankings' can involve the incorporation of the body and its products into images and video designed to shock and fascinate. These practices of self-exploitation can come full circle and ultimately breach normative expectations about 'authenticity' in social life, potentially triggering abuse and harassment.

This chapter suggests that the collision between social media visibility and social norms is particularly acute for girls and women. It begins by questioning the degree of scrutiny that attends girls and women's online practices and, in particular, the shaming of girls and women who are accused of 'doing it for attention'; that is, deploying their bodies in the production of social media content. This is contrasted with the absence of moral categories and judgements for male social media users who expose their bodies for admiration and comparison with others. Images of male bodies circulate on social media without arousing the controversy that attends female images, to the point where boys and men can use their bodies to produce and distribute deliberately crude and offensive images with few negative consequences. The chapter goes on to examine how this gendered asymmetry impacts on the exchange of intimate images within heterosexual relations. It shows how the production and exchange of 'nudes' or eroticised images is often characterised by a lack of reciprocity and mutual desire, and occurs with an online visual economy in which 'nudes' of girls and women are conflated with pornography. The chapter suggests that widespread and normalised differentials in gendered power blur the boundaries between the consensual and coerced exchange of intimate images, providing the 'cultural scaffolding' (Gavey, 2005) for online abuse.

'Doing it for attention': public femininity on social media

In focus groups, the activities and self-presentation of girls and young women on social media were a frequent topic of discussion. Both male and female participants expressed concern about 'naïve' younger sisters and cousins who placed images of themselves in 'sexy' clothing on social media, and were generally critical of girls and women seen to be capitalising upon their appearance online. Young people felt that the public display of female sexuality through provocative online images and social media content was not only unsafe but 'unhealthy' in the sense that a 'confident' woman does need to incite male desire to feel good about herself. Young women were often keen to distance themselves from such activity. Stephanie made a clear normative distinction between her modest 'confident' comportment and her friends who have a 'need' to 'show off' their bodies:

> I'm very conscious of the way I dress as well, whereas I know some of my friends will go out and wear as short as you can go and as high as you can wear. I don't know, maybe it's a thing of being comfortable with who you are. I don't feel like I need to show off my legs or my breasts or whatever to be confident in who I am.

Pejorative assessments of girls and women who 'show off' on social media or elsewhere were counterbalanced with assertions that women have a 'right' to 'wear short skirts and wear what they want without being judged'. This apparent contradiction emerges from the coexistence of irreconcilable codes of public femininity: one that warns girls and women away from being 'too' assertive or sexualised in public, and another that conflates sexualised self-display with female empowerment. Traditional presentations of the public/private divide conflated with 'separate spheres' of feminine privacy and male publicity have been destabilised by feminist activism, and the partial integration of feminist sentiment within consumer and pop culture (McRobbie, 2008). The emergence of 'new vocabularies of representations of women as active, desiring subjects' has placed considerable focus on slender youthful bodies as an important element of femininity, and the display of this body is understood as 'powerful and playful rather than passive or victimized' (Gill, 2008: 43). At the same time, a powerful discourse about the premature 'sexualisation' of girls within a 'pornographied' consumer culture re-pathologises sexualised display amongst adolescent girls as 'at risk' and dangerous behaviour (Lumby and Albury, 2010).

Young people tended to endorse the viability of a sexualised public femininity in theory, but this was contradicted by their expectations of girls and women in everyday life. Regardless of the messages of consumer culture, modesty, affability and 'fitting in' continue to be highly valued personal feminine attributes (Ringrose, 2013: 90). Being 'too' visible or 'too' sexy on social media could transgress those values, triggering blame and judgement. In the excerpt below, Keslee criticises a younger female cousin for posting a photo of herself in a bikini to Facebook:

KESLEE: My cousin is 14 or 15, she has a picture of herself standing up in the bath, wet with like a bikini on, and the guys on her Facebook – this is the thing, it's ridiculous, and that's why they're doing it as well. And all the guys are, 'Oh you little hottie, oh I love you', and she glows.

ROB: Well, that is the only time you see 950 likes and whatever.

ANDREA: Yeah, they're doing it for attention.

'Doing it for attention' was, for young people, a broad category of motive that described any girl or woman deemed to be exposing her body on social media to garner male admiration. In the exchange above, young people recognised that images of youthful feminine bodies have a particular cultural currency on social media ('that is the only time you see 950 likes') but their focus is not on the peer or media context in which attention is prioritised to her body but rather on her choice to make the image available. The constrained choices available to the young female social media user – 'modest' obscurity or 'immodest' notoriety – are eclipsed by a highly moralistic focus on personal responsibility for girls and women. This focus pervaded peer, educational and familial contexts. Teachers and parents were at pains to foreground modesty and restraint as the guiding principles of femininity. Robyn recalled:

I went to an all-girls school, so we had those whole [talks about] 'Your body is your temple, girls'. You never hear of guys having that education […] Just once every few months, the whole grade would be put into a group and they'd go, 'You're all special, your bodies are temples, respect yourselves, girls'. Like you don't get guys being spoken to in those soft, velvety tones.

The characterisation of the feminine body as a 'temple' or object of specific veneration does not disallow feminine sexuality but rather disciplines it in specific ways. Imbuing the feminine body as the receptacle of 'respect' carries the implication that the sanctity of the body, and by extension the respectable self, is at risk from indiscriminate sexuality. Ostensibly positive ideals of feminine 'self-respect' and healthy sexual development thus contain a more traditional focus on the importance of maintaining a reputation unsullied by inopportune sexual contact. Such discourses tend to conflate consensual and non-consensual sexual experiences, since they are both construed as besmirching the reputation of the girl. Contemporary 'cyber-safety' messages and education campaigns reinforce this by emphasising the 'foolishness' of girls who take and share intimate images, foregrounding their shame and loss of social standing (Salter et al., 2013).

'Cyber-safety' efforts often aimed to protect girls from themselves as much as from others. Parental anxiety about the internet activities of their daughters could drive the invasion of their privacy and justify the strict regulation of their conduct online and offline. In Lucy's experience, her parents' surveillance of her phone and computer was so intrusive that it had ongoing consequences for her relationship with them:

> When I was in high school my parents went through my text messages and my emails and it really destroyed our relationship and it's still something that is an issue, it's something I can't really get over – there was a time when my parents just went a little bit crazy, it was just really intense. That was something I could never forgive them for, I was only 16 or something.

Chris commented specifically on the restrictions placed on his older sister's use of the internet, which he situated within a broader regime of control over her life:

> My dad's pretty hard-core. My sister's three years older than me and she couldn't go on [chat rooms and social media] or whatever, but I could do whatever I wanted, because it comes down to sex again. My dad – 'cause my sister's a girl, he wants to know where she's going, when she's coming back, whereas, me, it was just like, 'Go do what you want'.

For Chris, his father's prescriptions surrounding his sister's online activities were congruent with his close monitoring of her more generally. Guarding daughters from exposure to sex or sexuality under the guise of 'protecting' them is a long-standing parental prerogative. Importantly, the reputations of girls and young women were not considered their property but rather multiple adults and institutions had a stake in it, including families, schools and churches who were anxious that girls' online activities did not bring them into disrepute by association. For instance, Toni was raised by her parents within an evangelical Christian community. While she retained a strong sense of religious conviction and belonging, she was outraged when her church collectively condemned her for a photo she uploaded to Facebook. In the following excerpt, she described her sense of shock and betrayal as she realised that her Facebook profile was being monitored by her priest, who instructed her to remove an image that he felt was giving people 'the wrong idea' about her.

TONI: [In the photo] I was sitting on the floor and the guy was like throwing the whole contents [of a bottle of alcohol] in my mouth. That was a good photo and then I uploaded it on Facebook and all hell went loose. I had to go to church, and then we had this meeting, and the priest came up to me and he's like, 'That photo's not a very conservative photo.' I'm like, 'I love that photo. I'm not removing it.' He's like, 'It just gives people the wrong idea of you.' I'm like, 'Why are you looking into my Facebook? What has this come down to?' He's like, 'Look sister, maybe you shouldn't add photos like this.' 'No I like it.' 'It's not a very appropriate photo,' and I'm like, 'I'll decide what's appropriate,' and then he's like, 'Well…'. He started becoming religious [at me]. Are you serious? It came down to the point that – our community's very small and tight, but it comes to a point where people point their nose in other people's business. That was none of his business. I'm not removing it. He's like, 'Why?'

FACILITATOR: How did he come across your profile at all?

TONI: I don't know, but the problem is the fact that he sits there and thinks he has the right to tell me to remove it. That really upset me. Then even some people, 'It [the image] looks mad.' That was offending. I really liked it. I was going to throw up loads [and take a photo of it and put it online] just to piss the guy off.

As previous chapters have argued, the architecture of social media rewards the kinds of outrageous or edgy images that Toni describes above. A photo of a girl or woman on the floor with her mouth open as a man pours alcohol over her is likely to attract more attention, 'likes' and comments than the kinds of 'conservative' images that her priest preferred. Toni's 'good photo' displays a kind of female abandon that is celebrated within popular culture as pleasurable and liberating. It corresponds closely with the advertising and viral strategies of the alcohol industry in its efforts to encourage young people to generate and upload images of alcohol consumption to social media (Brodmerkel and Carah, 2013). However, as Toni's experience shows, there can be a significant gap between what constitutes a salient feminine display on social media and the expectations of families and communities.

These contradictory expectations were a particular challenge for girls and women who belonged to cultural and religious communities in which female conduct is linked to familial and community honour. There were clear elements of these traditions in Toni's account, against which she fiercely mobilised notions of individual self-determination and autonomy. However, these concepts are not equally salient or available to all girls and women, particularly in community contexts where the slightest perception of sexual impropriety could have explosive consequences for the girl and her family. Anisa recalled an incident in her high school when she was 13 or 14 in which a teenaged boy shamed a female classmate by circulating a picture she had sent to him. In her cultural community, which she described as 'Middle Easternish', Anisa said that the prevailing view was that girls 'should be staying at home' and should not be seen to be involved with boys in any way. A classmate broke this rule when she sent a photo of herself to a boy which, while certainly not nude or overtly sexualised, was considered to be 'showing a lot of skin' according to community standards. The boy then 'sent it to everyone', triggering controversy within the school and community.

> No-one ever blamed the guy. Even when I was talking to my family they go, 'It's her fault, she shouldn't have sent it', which is true but I feel like the humiliation – he didn't even, nothing happened to him. He was older than her. I think the police called on him or something but nothing, no-one blamed him. They

were like, 'It's alright, you didn't do anything wrong'. That's how it was treated. Where I come from, they have this very sexist, unmodernised view of women and women get blamed a lot for stuff like that.

In this excerpt, Anisa accepts that it was 'true' that the girl 'shouldn't have sent it' (the photo) but questioned the sole attribution of culpability to the girl, which she viewed as 'sexist, unmodernised'. The boy may have received a cautionary visit from the police but was, in Anisa's account, otherwise exculpated of responsibility. Instead she felt her community mobilised against the girl in order to affirm standards of feminine modesty, impacting on the social standing not only of the girl but also of her family. For Anisa, this incident illustrated the challenges that faced girls in her community reconciling the discontinuity between what she called the 'unmodern' views of parents and kin (often recent migrants and refugees) and the rituals of 'modern' courtship and sociability. She described quietly policing her social media profile so as not to upset her mother:

My mum, she usually doesn't like me hanging out in groups of guys and girls, which doesn't stop me because I don't see that there's a problem with it… This girl, she took a photo on her iPhone, she tagged me in it but the photo – for my mum who is a really conservative woman, she wouldn't like to see a photo of me sitting on a bed with one girl and four other guys even if one of them was my brother. If my mum wouldn't like something like that, I'm usually careful to make sure nothing like that ever goes online.

Although the policing of female online conduct is more intensive in some households and communities than others, there was a continuity between Anisa's experience and those of other young women that challenges the linear arrangement of gendered attitudes from 'unmodern' to 'modern'. Instead, girls and young women were disciplined in incongruous ways to present themselves as demure embodiments of feminine modesty and as transgressing those same norms through sexualised and daring displays of autonomy. The line of delineation between 'good' and 'bad' femininity was unclear but closely scrutinised by parents, teachers and peers. In contrast, as the next section suggests, the online behaviour of boys and young men came with considerably lessened anxieties about reputational impacts, to the point where male users could engage in crude displays with a relative sense of impunity. These activities sometimes involved forms of bodily exposure and nudity that would have had serious consequences if undertaken by a girl or woman. However, a prevailing ethos of 'boys will be boys' gives male online vulgarity a sympathetic or even approving reception amongst bystanders. This demonstrates the uneven standing of male and female users online, particularly in the production and exchange of digital images so crucial to social media participation and, often, intimate relationships.

Pranks, gym selfies and male bodily display

The ways in which young people deployed their bodies in online images, and the manner in which those images were circulated and interpreted, varied considerably according to gender. Amongst some young men, there was a resistance to the objectification of their own body or other male bodies through photography. Self-photos or 'selfies' had an air of vanity that was considered un-masculine. Pejorative mass media and online descriptions of the 'selfie' associate it with female narcissism and thus frame it as an inappropriate activity for male users (Burns, 2015). Instead, young men suggested that they were more likely to use photos to document themselves socialising or 'pranking' others.

NICK: I haven't taken a photo in months, so I don't know. You don't really see much guy photos put up though.
LOUISE: I think it's not common for guys to take selfies, because some guys just don't like photos at all.
SERGIO: Or if they have photos, it's like they're either drinking or with friends or something like that.
NICK: Or they do selfies to take the piss out of other people.
SERGIO: Yeah.

In this exchange, young people described how men and boys used photos on social media to enhance the visibility of various masculine activities, such as drinking or 'taking the piss' (an Australian colloquialism for making fun of others). At times, 'taking the piss' on social media had a collaborative aspect in which the person targeted cooperates with the friends making fun of him. For example, Mark described a Facebook acquaintance whose social media profile was, in Mark's words, regularly 'raped' by his friends, meaning that they would 'change the photos to disgusting things'.

MARK: Yeah, yeah there's one guy it happens all the time.

FACILITATOR: Alright so someone – people have hacked into his Facebook?

MARK: Or he's just left it on and they've gone onto it and found the most disgusting thing they can find and changed his pictures.

FACILITATOR: Okay, so more detail, example, like what would they change his profile pictures to?

MARK: One of them was a naked really old black woman and it was just not desirable.

FACILITATOR: So why does it keep happening to him?

MARK: I don't know, it's just his mates I think.

Mark's cavalier use of the term 'rape' and his suggestion that a 'naked really old black woman' is the 'most disgusting thing' is indicative of cultural logics of sexism, racism and ageism that are pervasive both in juvenile male peer groups and in many online contexts. This combination of masculine hedonism, exhibitionism and prejudice has been theorised as a subtle form of sexist hostility 'masquerading as irony and pastiche' (Attwood, 2006: 83). It functions to affirm male peer groups through the public airing of deliberately vulgar sentiments, much in the way the language of abuse and insult was used to discursively police the boundaries of 4chan (see Chapter 2). The boy in question could bring a stop to this activity simply by changing his password, and the fact that he doesn't suggests a level of complicity and enjoyment of the ongoing prank. In her study of British teenagers, Livingstone (2008: 399) described a similar situation in which a 13-year-old boy shared his Myspace password with his brothers and friends who regularly changed the information on his profile for fun. Livingstone (2008) notes that his profile acts as a nexus of sociality that displays to others 'his lively and trusting relations with his brothers and friends' (p. 400).

These examples are notable for the relative freedom from scrutiny and judgement that attended male self-representations online. Revealing or offensive images and profiles could be incorporated into shared forms of homosocial play that were likely to be understood as such by participants and bystanders, even if they found them offensive. The potential implications of posting pornography to Facebook (which is certainly a breach of the site's terms of service, and likely to be objectionable to other users) or circulating a naked photo of a 'guy smashed [drunk] doing a strip [running naked] all the way down the road' are elided within a shared camaraderie. The abandon with which male social media users could create and share images of their body was particularly striking. Young people described male bodies as normalised parts of the public landscape, to be exposed and used at will in comparison to the female bodies that needed to be kept covered and secret. Alicia commented:

> Yeah, guys walk around topless, that's normal so there's not much else you can really show without a picture, so if you get a topless photo of your girl, it's a big deal, where if it's a guy it's like, whatever you can walk on the beach in board shorts, so it's not that different to what you would see in public anyway.

Some young women expressed exasperation and amazement at the apparent impunity from humiliation that boys and men enjoyed online while female users were expected to carefully curate and monitor their social media presence to ensure it was free from any hint of impropriety. Ellen recalled:

> One of my friends was peeing and took a picture of himself 'cause he thought it was funny and sent it to his friend, and then his friend – all his guy friends have this picture of him. I've seen it, but they think it's funny – I don't know, that's kind of the case. He doesn't care, he was like 'I took it, I don't care'.

Hope describes a similar incident in high school in which a male student circulated a photo of his genitals to the entire school bus. She noted the very different consequences such behaviour would have had for a girl:

Once when I was in year 11, I was sitting on the school bus going home and I had my Bluetooth turned on and so did a bunch of other girls and boys around me. This message came and a guy was like, 'Oh receive it, it's really funny,' and I opened it and it was a picture of the genitals of the guy sitting next to me.

They were just both smiling and laughing and all these kids on the bus had a picture of his penis. It wasn't embarrassing for them. He thought it was hilarious but if a girl's vagina, a picture of that was sent around that would not be seen in the same way. She probably wouldn't do it to begin with as a generalisation and it wouldn't be funny. It would be harmful for her. It would be seen as like really brazen and negative.

Hope was troubled by the double standard evident in the incident she witnessed, and Ellen was incredulous that a photo of her male friend urinating could be considered 'funny'. These acts were simply unthinkable for young women who felt that the consequences for them would be 'harmful' and 'negative'. While girls and women may ape and grimace for the camera in deliberately grotesque ways (Dobson, 2014), they cannot expose their naked body online without considerable backlash. Meanwhile, boys and men engaged in a range of antics 'for attention' online, up to and including the circulation of pornography and the exposure of their genitals. This was variously interpreted as 'funny', crude and shocking but it did not spark the same kind of speculation about psychological health, self-esteem and self-respect that surrounded girls who 'do it for attention'. Their online displays of their bodies and sexuality were not considered to be discontinuous with normative masculinity.

This was true even in the case of the 'gym selfie', where boys and men breached gendered prescriptions against male 'selfies' by taking topless photos of themselves and posting them to social media to display their 'gains' (or muscular development from weight lifting). When asked about the motivations behind the 'gym selfie', one group of young men said:

ROB: It's kind of to let everyone see how big you are.
NICHOLAS: Yeah, so they usually take a photo in a mirror or something and it's them flexing or something at the gym.

FACILITATOR: And is this taken for the girls, or is it taken kind of as a competition between guys?

ROB: For attention as well.

STEPHEN: I guess it's both and to say they're going to the gym so that people know.

ROB: To show off their [muscular] gains.

JULIAN: Yeah. Pretty much.

Girls and women who exposed their bodies 'for attention' online are often accused of 'cheapening' themselves by forgoing 'respect' and instead playing to rapacious male sexuality (Burns, 2015). Boys and men who engage in equivalent practices were largely immune from such judgements. There was some expression of concern for the makers of gym selfies: Stephen criticised 'pop culture' for telling young men that 'you need to be ripped' [muscular and skinny], and Ben described how the focus on 'abs and muscles and all that stuff' had led some of his friends to begin taking steroids. Absent from these discussions was any particularly strong condemnation of the boys and men who make them. These images were at times gently mocked as overly narcissistic, and other researchers have observed men and boys shaming or 'unfollowing' male users who make 'selfies' of their bodies on social media (Williams and Marquez, 2015). However, in contrast to girls and women, exposing their bodies for attention did not brand boys and men as a particular 'type' of male who, by definition, deserves ostracism and public humiliation. Nor were 'gym selfies' discussed as the source of parental anxiety or school intervention. The supposed vanity of the 'gym selfie' might be amusing but it didn't require intervention and regulation on par with that endured by young women. Indeed, concerns about the health and wellbeing of boys online did not pertain to their own behaviour per se but rather to potential corruption or manipulation by girls and women. Suspicion that girls and women 'use' their bodies on and off social media in order to control males surfaced in various ways throughout the focus groups. As the next section examines, this was grounded in an approach to heterosexual relations that generally held girls and women to be more sexually agentic and calculating than boys and men, and therefore responsible when they are the target of online abuse.

The exchange of 'nudes' in intimate relations

The gendered assymetry in the online visual economy was particularly apparent in the exchange of sexualised or nude images. This is sometimes known as 'sexting', although young people in this study usually called these images 'nudes'. In an intimate relationship, 'nudes' could be part of a mutually desired exchange, such as in the case of Wendy:

> I was in a relationship for just over a year and a half and went to school together... For the last three months of the relationship we were in different states so after a year and a half together there's trust. Still a bit of travelling backwards and forwards as much was realistic but yeah, definitely sexting. I think it's still a form of intimacy no matter how distant that might be. It's still that form of intimacy.

The exchange of intimate images is becoming an increasingly normalised aspect of intimate and sexual relations. A representative sample of young American adults found that one-third had sent a nude or semi-nude image of themselves to another person (AP/MTV, 2009) and surveys based on convenience samples suggest that up to half of adults have done the same (Klettke et al., 2014). In the era of online dating sites, making and sending nude images has become part of the sexual repertoire of large numbers of adults. Wendy gives an account of this characterised by reciprocal trust and desire. Such reciprocity was largely absent in most descriptions of exchanging 'nudes' and sexting amongst teenagers. It was more typical for young people to discuss boys requesting 'nudes' from girls, who provide these images in the hope that the boy will initiate or maintain a relationship with her. Alicia said:

> The experiences that I know about of people, it's been the girl to the guy. It's never been the other way, and in one of the cases, the grade younger than mine, the girl sent it to the guy and they weren't going out, but she wanted to go out with him so it was a weird way of saying 'I'm into you' sort of thing, so I think the way that girls think about this and guys think about it is different.
>
> I think, just from my opinion, it's more like the guys expect the girls will send it kind of thing, instead of saying it's reciprocal, it's

more the girls will send it and the guys will be like, whatever, but they won't send one back if that makes sense. So I feel like, from what little experience I know about, it's been the one way transmission rather than the mutual thing that you would expect in an established couple if that makes sense.

By and large, accounts of 'nudes' or sexting conformed to the notion that heterosexuality is structured around an 'economy of sex' in which girls and women exchange sex for intimacy and commitment (Gavey, 2005: 141). Young people recognised that girls and women can be sexually interested in the naked form, but female desire was largely missing in their descriptions of producing and exchanging intimate images. This 'missing discourse of desire' (Fine, 1988) does not signal that girls and women don't experience pleasure in the exchange of images, but rather that many of these exchanges were not orientated around and towards female desire. Instead, young people described dynamics of image production that cleaved more closely to a 'different and unequal' model of sexuality (Gavey, 2005: 117). Women feature in this model not as desiring subjects but in the more traditional sense as responsible for the satisfaction of male desire and keeping men 'happy'. Young women worried that refusing to provide a 'nude' to their partner might be misconstrued as an expression of distrust that could destabilise the relationship. Kate said:

I know girls that have been shamed and blamed by their boyfriends for failing to deliver on this image. I know girls that, you know if the guys didn't have it [a nude], they would sulk and would say 'Don't you see I'm doing this out of love for you, I just appreciate you, I love your body, I want to have a keepsake of it', and these girls would really feel upset at themselves for not doing it.

Such accounts trouble the notion of sexting within relationships as a harmless intimate practice or sexual aid, and instead emphasise how sexual negotiations within relationships are shaped by gendered discourses and norms that place women and girls under considerable pressure to acquiesce to sexual activity they might otherwise prefer to avoid. In relation to the provision of 'nudes', this 'normalisation of sexual compliance' (Burkett and Hamilton, 2012: 825) places girls and women at potential risk, particularly once a relationship has ended. This is captured in a focus group exchange that began with Andrea describing a recent dilemma facing her friend:

ANDREA: My friend and her boyfriend recently broke up at the end of last semester, and he kind of went a little bit crazy trying to get her back. He had pictures, not that she had sent him, but while they were together that he took of her.

LAURA: Consensually?

ANDREA: Consensually. But he was like saying that he was going to spread them around, he just kind of went off the deep end. I remember I was with her and she was literally hysterically crying because she didn't even send him that picture, he took it himself – even though it was consensual but she was just so worried that everyone would see it because that would be devastating for her.

KESLEE: So it sounds like a power play, but it always seems to be the male over the female.

BECKY: Yeah like 'I have this picture of you I can use whenever I want to'.

ALISON: So then we're back to – guys don't care, guys, you'll have a dick pic, [you say] 'I'm going to send that', [but he says] 'okay good, show everyone'.

Alison's point is that men and women who have exchanged or manufactured 'nudes' together are not equally vulnerable to humiliation if the other party decides to show the image to others. The non-consensual publication of a nude image is less consequential for a man than a woman. After the relationship that Andrea described ended, the male partner 'went off the deep end' claiming he would 'spread than around' (photos of his now ex-partner). Alison observed that this threat could not be reciprocated by the woman even if she had intimate images of the man in her possession. The man could reasonably say, 'Okay good, show everyone', because the circulation of his 'nude' was unlikely to have particularly negatively ramifications for him. Andrew agreed that male nudity can be 'whatever' but publicised female nudity means 'slut':

> I think that's why it's so embarrassing [for girls] because the guys
> are 'whatever' [about their own nudity], if a guy sends a picture of
> a girl around it's like 'oh, look at her, she's a slut, she sent a naked
> picture', and then it becomes even more embarrassing because you
> don't just hear 'naked', now you think 'she's a slut'.

In effect, two interlinked forms of gender inequality shaped the
exchange of 'nudes' in intimate relations. The first involved hegemonic
sexual scripts that prioritised male sexual desire as the fulcrum of heterosexual relations. The second involved the pejorative signification of
female 'nudes' on social media as synonymous with brazen promiscuity
and sexual deviance. While girls and women were aware that supplying
a 'nude' placed them at risk of public humiliation, denying a request for
such an image was disruptive to sexual and gendered scripts in which
'good' femininity is predicated on compliance. This is a new iteration
of the familiar double bind that girls should not be too 'slutty' but
should also not be 'prudes' (Tolman, 2002: 119 and 120). The conflation
of public female nudity with the 'slut' was ubiquitous in focus group
discussions about girls and women on social media. The next section
discusses how young women's conduct was framed in focus groups
within a transactional model in which they were frequently criticised
for exchanging their bodies for 'attention'.

Sluts, attention whores and the stigma of the prostitute

In European culture, the counterpoint to the 'good' chaste woman
who minds her place in the private sphere is the allegedly promiscuous
and deviant 'public' woman or prostitute (Landes, 1998). While the
phrase 'public man' describes a male figure of authority, the term
'public woman' has historically been an 'epithet for one who was seen
as the dregs of society, vile, unclean' and synonymous with prostitution
(Matthews, 1992: 4). The label of 'slut' has long been deployed in the
regulation of female sexuality and public representation (Attwood,
2007). The regularity with which female public figures are degraded on
social media as 'sluts' and other sexually visceral insults is indicative of
the continuity of this ideology to the present day. So too is the term
'attention whores' used by young people to describe girls and women

who make 'nude' images of themselves. Lana was particularly out-spoken on this issue, decrying 'attention whores' who cynically lure men using the power of the 'nude'. She said:

> It's also usually girls that can't get boys, not because of their looks, but they just don't get boys. They do it for attention, because that's what attracts boys I suppose, they love all that dirty stuff.

Lana suggests that some girls, in an effort to 'get boys', provide 'nudes' in a deliberate attempt to attract them with 'dirty stuff'. This has strong pejorative overtones. Characterising girls who make 'nudes' as both desperate 'for attention' and calculating in their pursuit of it rationalises their subsequent derogation as 'attention whores' and objects of ridicule. This is a view that renders irrelevant the question of whether the 'nude' came to public attention because it was circulated without her consent. As Dobson (2015: 92, emphasis in original) observes, 'girls who were seen to "seek attention" via either publicly posted *or privately shared* body or heterosexy self-images were also perceived as *culpable* for any harassment or bullying that eventuated from the misuse of their images by others'. Tara provided a more reflective account of the term 'attention whore' and the way that it obscures male perpetration and justifies the shaming of female victims of online abuse.

> My friends I think, most of my peers would use [the term] 'attention whoring'. Basically they see it as an excuse to get attention, by sending nudes, particularly – particularly girls, I don't know why, it's always girls that gets looked down on. If a girl sends a nude picture of herself, of, say, her breasts to her boyfriend, with both parties consenting and they break-up and the boyfriend releases that picture online, or something along those lines, the girl is seen as attention whoring, as in she's 'begging for attention', when she's saying 'No, I don't want this, this is between me and my ex, not online', kind of thing.

'Attention whore' captured the transactional nature by which girls and women are deemed to come to male attention: namely, through the provocative display of their own body and sexuality. The phrase rests on the assumption that self-exploitation is the most available mode by which girls and women can escape the quietude of appropriate femininity and become 'noticed' by men and boys, albeit at considerable cost to their reputation. Men and boys who take risks 'for attention' are rarely if ever described as 'attention whores', and their antics are generally ascribed to masculine boisterousness or their 'inability to be tamed' (Moore, 2013). Commenting on this evident double standard in pop culture, journalist Moore (2013) says:

> No matter that Charlie Sheen, James Franco and Scott Disick litter the landscape – those are 'bad boys'. Attention whore is a term mostly reserved for women – sad, fucked up women who deserve every last little fleck of spit we project their way.

While the label 'attention whore' can be ascribed to any girl or woman deemed to be too invested in attracting (specifically male) attention, it had an additional resonance when applied to the 'nude', since it positioned the 'image' as a form of pornography and its subject, by implication, as a prostitute. Trish recognised that the provision of a 'nude' could be understood as an act of 'devotion' in an intimate relationship, but she also felt that it bestowed the power on the male partner to 'turn you into what these girls are in the porn industry'. If he chose to make the image public, then he was effectively characterising the girl as a sex worker or prostitute.

> For a woman, it's this really personal thing to reveal herself to a man in this private setting and on that basis of that devotion, 'yes, you can have it' [a sexy photo], it's like a gift. And then for that to become 'I'm going to turn you into what these girls in the porn industry are without your consent'.

There was no clear line of delineation between the 'nude' and pornography in young people's descriptions and experiences. The same technological advances that have enabled the self-production and circulation of private images have also provided unprecedented access to pornography. 'Nudes' were made and circulated on the same devices and computers that could be used to access and share pornography. Indeed, there are now numerous websites and social media accounts that exist to circulate self-produced 'nudes', and it's likely that most of these images are shared without the permission of the person depicted. For young women, the spectre of such sexual exploitation hung over their use of camera and internet technology in intimate relations, imbuing the potentially desirable or pleasurable act of image exchange with intractable risks. In the discussion below, Becky and Kate situated the production of images of male and female nudity within the double standards that inhere in pornography and in society in general. Becky argues that in such a context, the self-manufacture of a nude image by a girl or woman is indelibly linked to self-'pornographising':

BECKY: I imagine a naked picture of yourself, I know there's not a verb for this, but you're like pornographising yourself. I think it's basically saying I'm going to be porn for you basically. I mean you would never find out about some guy – say you found out some guy was in a porn film, I just don't think it would be defamatory to his character. But if people found out that a girl had been in a porn film I think it really would. So maybe we want to get to a stage where girls don't care if a naked picture of themselves get spread around. But I think women are so conscious of their bodies and so conscious of their role as sexual that it's going to be really hard to get to that spot because they really want to control how they're seen sexually and to have yourself used as eye candy for a whole community of people…

KATE: I don't think it's that men aren't – they do have inhibitions about their body and about how they are seen sexually, it's just that women have this term slut next to their name quite often.

The allegation that girls and women depicted in 'nudes' are 'whores' or 'sluts' is not only a misogynist slur, but it touches on the ways in which newly available forms of sexual representation in intimate relations, such as 'nudes', blur into the products of the sex industry. Becky describes a friend who was placed under pressure by her boyfriend to provide him with a 'nude' as substitute masturbatory material:

BECKY: I've had a couple of friends who've done it [provided their boyfriend with a 'nude'] and what they say is – one of them was like 'I know my boyfriend looks at porn, I know he needs porn to masturbate, and he's saying to me, "What am I meant to do? I need to masturbate and I want to masturbate over you, so please we have sex I see you all the time, I just want that so I can keep that in my personal home".'

ROB: Convenience.

BECKY: [The boyfriend says] 'So I'm extending our sexual congress in the privacy of my own home, you don't want me to have to masturbate over these women'. She said 'No of course not, if I'm willing to show you me naked any time without photographic record then it's just an extension of that'. She thought it was this loving thing, like a gift, she was enabling his sexuality and making sure it was directed towards her.

Male sexual desire is constructed in this quote as an irrepressible urge that includes a 'need' for pornography. The request for a 'nude' is thus framed as a supplicatory appeal from the boy to the girl to help him satiate his uncontrollable desires with an image of her. This either/or proposition places the girl in a dilemma: *either* she provides him with the image he demands *or* he has no choice but to continue masturbating to internet pornography. Her role as his girlfriend is envisioned as 'enabling' and 'directing' his sexuality in more respectable, monogamous ways. However, the status of the 'nude' as a devotional 'gift' or marital aid is contingent on the relational context in which is made. Becky described her friend's ongoing anxiety over the status of this image a few years after the end of the relationship, knowing that the image can be easily reframed as the very pornography it was designed to supplant.

When they broke up, she was absolutely terrified, and two years later she said to me – last week, she said, 'I just keep thinking, he can sit in his room any time within the next 50 years and double click on that file and I know he hasn't deleted it, and he can masturbate over it, he can show it to anyone he wants. We don't like one another so what guarantee do I have?' She said 'I will never be at peace about this'. And so many girls do that.

Both partners are aware that, outside the relationship, the 'nude' takes on a derogatory power and becomes indistinguishable from pornography. This interpretation of the image is all the more potent in the scenario described by Becky because the 'nude' was manufactured as a pornography substitute in the first place. It is notable that there was no mention of the boy reciprocating with an image of his own. Instead, his ownership of the 'nude' bequeaths him with considerable power over an ex-partner. This includes the ongoing threat of publicising the image without her consent. However, she was deeply uncomfortable with the proposition that he might privately continue to view the image for sexual pleasure. Both acts have an objectifying dimension that young women could find threatening and offensive.

The tendency of girls and women to turn the camera towards their bodies, and for boys and men to turn the camera away from their own, is commensurate with well-established feminist critiques of female objectification and the male gaze (e.g. Mulvey, 1999). In this process, men and boys are positioned as desiring subjects and girls and women as desired objects. A request for a 'nude' not only put girls and women at risk of being shamed and humiliated, but young women felt it positioned them as a sexual object within the relationship rather than an equal partner. For some, this was a serious insult. One young woman was particularly clear about the probable ramifications of such a request in her current relationship:

> I'd go off at my boyfriend if he asked for one [a nude image]. 'You asked for what?!' I'd seriously go off. I'd go off. He just wouldn't dare ask something like that from me. If he said that to me all hell would go loose.

Attwood (2006: 83) argues that it is important to examine 'how an active female sexuality can be materialized in culture' and this was a particular issue that young people struggled with. While young people generally endorsed ideals of active female sexual desire and agency, these ideals were contradicted by their lived experience of negotiating intimate relations. In this study, young women and men affirmed the importance of female sexual desire and pleasure but nonetheless described the exchange of 'nudes' according to polarised sexual scripts. Men and boys felt entitled to ask for and expect 'nudes' from girls and women, who sometimes felt that they did not have the right to decline, but bore all the risks of this exchange should the image be made public. When such an image is non-consensually circulated, the intention or context behind the manufacture of the image was lost as the meaning of the image was over-written by the pervasive figure of the 'slut' or 'whore' as the most available symbol to describe any form of feminine sexual self-display, and particularly those made public.

Conclusion

This chapter argues that the online visual economy is structured by significant gendered differentials in power. On social media, a range of subject positions were available to men and boys while femininity was constructed according to simplistic dichotomies. Online, boys and men could identify themselves as friends, brothers, pranksters, drinking buddies and so on. The knowing self-objectification of the 'gym selfie' does not displace or eclipse these alternative masculine postures but rather emerges as an alternative form of masculine display. In contrast, a conservative sexual morality provided the hegemonic organising principles around which girls and women's online presentation was assessed and judged. In focus groups, the ideal of the confident girl who does not need to expose her body for validation online was persistently contrasted with the 'immature', 'naïve' girl who trades on her sexuality on social media. This represents a continuation of older and entrenched norms of feminine modesty and privacy in direct conflict with more recent configurations of femininity as sexualised, empowered and hyper-visible (Gill, 2008). The long-standing pejorative stereotype of the sexually promiscuous 'public woman' has been recuperated in some quarters of youth and consumer culture as an expression of female autonomy and advancement (McRobbie, 2008). However, schools, families and peers still strictly enforced traditional standards of modesty and propriety upon girls and women, who appeared caught between contradictory norms of sexual 'assertiveness' and modesty.

Gendered differentials in power and sexual scripting in the manufacture and exchange of 'nude' images creates a continuum of coercion that may stop short of outright abuse but nonetheless prefigures and creates the context in which abuse is more likely. These include circumstances in which girls and women felt obliged to provide an image to a male partner in the hope of maintaining his interest, or, once in a relationship, she went along with online practices that she neither desired nor enjoyed, because she didn't feel it was her right to stop it and didn't know how to refuse. These findings are congruent with research that suggests that a significant proportion of young women's early sexual experiences take place outside the bounds of mutual desire and enthusiasm (Holland et al., 1998; Tolman, 2002; Gavey, 2005). Optimistic hopes that social media will transform gender inequalities or generate new opportunities for female autonomy must contend the embeddedness of social media within intimate and peer relations where gender inequality remains a powerful force. Recent 'sexting scandals' in which high school students were found to be making, swapping and 'scoring' nude photos of classmates on a rating system, with the boy with the most pictures named 'pimp of the pictures', illustrates how the quantifying logics of social media intersects and gives shape to gendered social formations (Cloos and Turkewitz, 2015).

The analysis focuses in particular on young people's references to 'sluts' and 'whores' as insults directed at, and as categories of, female social media users, and the prescriptive power of the prostitute as a regulatory figure of female sexuality that endures, and is perhaps enhanced, in the era of online pornography. The figure of the prostitute has long been used to characterise public femininity as improper and immodest, to the point where the stigmatisation of sex work can potentially adhere to any girl or woman deemed too assertive in public or too flagrant in her sexual expression. The recurrence of this discriminatory trope on social media, encapsulated in the term 'attention whore', suggests an ongoing discomfort with girls and women who make use of the new forms of public and private expression enabled by online and digital technology. The ways in which nude or sexualised images of girls and women on social media can overlap with, and potentially be absorbed into, the online visual economy of pornography, was a particular point of frisson as young women could find their bodily images treated as interchangeable with the products of the sex industry. In contrast, male bodily exposure attracted considerably less pejorative associations, even in 'gym selfies' where boys and men pose and preen semi-nude for the camera. The different ways in which images of male and female bodies are situated and interpreted online has significant implications for the ways in which sexual agency can be reworked into projects of gendered oppression and domination. This is discussed in more detail in the next chapter.

Suggested links

Read an excerpt from Susan Sontag's 1977 book *On Photography* at www.susa nsontag.com/SusanSontag/books/onPhotographyExerpt.shtml.

This Buzzfeed article from Rossalyn Warren (Twitter: @RossalynWarren) describes the Twitter hashtag #ShirtlessShames2016, launched by Twitter user Lindsay (@CardsAgstHrsmt) to call attention to the hypocrisy of men who post shirtless photos of themselves to social media while 'shaming' women who share images of their bodies online: www.buzzfeed.com/rossalynwarren/shir tless-shamers.

Jezebel's Tracy Moore (Twitter: @iusedtobepoor) and RookieMag's Lebohang Masango (Tumblr: http://novaherself.tumblr.com) provide two critical commentaries on the gendered label of 'attention whore': http://jezebel. com/in-defense-of-the-attention-whore-509362561;   www.rookiemag.com/ 2013/05/shameless-women.

5

DICK PICS, SEXTING AND REVENGE PORN

Weaponising gendered power online

The previous chapter explored how male and female nudity is attributed differing significance on social media, with female nudity understood as narrowly pornographic and salacious in contrast to the more fluid interpretations and less intensive scrutiny of images of male bodies. This chapter demonstrates that these gendered differentials can be 'weaponised' by boys and men to affirm hierarchies of power and enact public performances of aggressive, sexually potent masculinity through the derogation of girls and women. It focuses on two key examples of online abuse, the first being abusive 'sexting' (sometimes known as 'revenge porn'). The second example, which has attracted less attention, is the non-consensual sending of 'dick pics', in which men send unwanted images of their genitals to girls and women. The chapter goes on to examine how young people conceptualised justice in their response to online abuse, which was characterised by a highly individualised discourse of choice that tended towards victim-blaming. Nonetheless, a number of scenarios were described in focus groups that foregrounded moments of conflict and potential change in the gendered dimensions of online abuse. The latter half of the chapter discusses everyday scenarios in which the constraints of intimate image exchange were challenged or transformed as young people negotiate, defend against and adapt to shifts in technologically mediated power relations.

The gendering of online abuse

The prevalence of online abuse and harassment and its differential impact on women has been evident since the internet's popularisation in the 1990s (Herring, 1993; Brail, 1996; Spender, 1996). Prior to social media, forms of online harassment reported by women included abusive or threatening emails, 'spamming' the victim with unwanted junk emails, sending them computer viruses or impersonating them. In the late 1990s, this was accompanied by warnings that online harassment was escalating to include acts of stalking and violence (Ellison, 2001). With the advent of social media, online abuse and harassment continues to be a highly gendered phenomenon (Citron, 2014). The language of insult and abuse is common on social media and encountered by a large proportion of users; however, women are more likely to experience more frequent and intrusive forms of abuse (Pew Research Centre, 2014). Terms such as 'whore', 'slut' and 'rape' are used routinely on Twitter which suggests that casual misogyny is a normalised part of the online lexicon for some users (Bartlett et al., 2014).

In her analysis, Jeong (2015) argues that the focus on the content of online abusive, specifically the use of insults and threats, overlooks its behavioural dimensions. Some of the most frightening and intrusive forms of online abuse do not involve abusive content per se, but rather dangerous kinds of behaviour such as the online distribution of personal and identifying information. Jeong (2015) writes that:

Harassing content and harassing behaviour of course overlap. Internet postings are both content and behaviour. But changing the lens can completely change your understanding. 'Someone called me a bitch on their blog' is different from, 'Someone has posted on their blog about how much they hate me, every day for about three months'. Both of these statements can be about the same situation, but one speaks through the lens of content, and the other through the lens of behaviour.

For example, when writing about the years of abuse she has endured from one user on Twitter, writer Imani Gandy (2014) describes not only his persistent use of racial and misogynist slurs, but how they are interwoven into an obsessive behavioural pattern. She says:

> For the past two years, I have been harassed by someone calling himself Assholster, an anonymous Twitter asshole who, on most days, creates up to ten different Twitter accounts just so he can hurl racist slurs at me: I'm a 'nigger,' I look 'niggery,' I haven't earned my 'nigger card,' I'm a 'pseudonigger,' 'fucking niggster,' or 'scab nigger.'
>
> If you winced when you read that list of slurs, imagine having them lobbed at you nearly every day for two years.

Gandy goes on to describe his fanatical monitoring of her Twitter account, his abuse of the people she communicates with on Twitter, and his dissemination of personal information about her. The full impact of this abuse can only be understood if Assholster's use of invective is situated within his intrusive and fixated conduct. Focusing on the content of abuse and overlooking its behavioural dimensions minimises the seriousness of online abuse and its consequences. The content of abuse can be shocking or insulting but the behavioural aspects of incidents of online abuse are key markers of invasiveness and potential harm. Boys and men report routine exposure to insult on social media but they are much less likely to experience the kinds of harassing behaviour – breaches of privacy, repetitive unwanted conduct, sexually aggressive advances – that marks the social media experience of many female users (Pew Research Centre, 2014).

In this process, personal characteristics are rearticulated as insults and woven into an ongoing pattern of frightening and intrusive conduct that can exert considerable effects on the lives of targets. These experiences are not limited to public figures or high-profile women but they include the incorporation of social media into patterns of sexual harassment at school and in other contexts. In focus groups, young people described how social media and other online technologies could be used by boys and men in the enactment of forms of gendered abuse and humiliation. The next two sections discuss the non-consensual circulation of 'nudes' (sometimes called non-consensual 'sexting' or 'revenge porn') and sending of 'dick pics'. Both of these cases involve sexualised content in the form of 'nude' images that takes on abusive qualities through its incorporation into practices of harassment and humiliation.

The non-consensual circulation of 'nudes'

Young people were familiar with a range of incidents in which nude or intimate photos were exploitatively solicited and then circulated via text message, email and social media. These incidents almost invariably involved boys and young men either seeking 'nudes' or eroticised images from girls and women or, in some cases, taking images and video without their consent. In the mass media, discussions about boys collecting nude images of girls and showing them to others are often framed in terms of the boy's emerging (hetero)sexuality and desire to view the naked female form. While young people agreed that boys and men probably enjoyed receiving and viewing these images, they emphasised factors other than sexual desire that prompted boys to solicit these images and show them to others without the consent of the girl. In particular, collecting 'nudes' of girls and women enabled a form of abusive homosociality in which boys and men distinguished themselves amongst their peers. Young people described groups of teenaged boys at high school clustered around each other's phones in a competitive display of their 'collections'.

ASHLEY: Because, with guys, all the other guys are like 'Wow, you've got so many photos'. Yeah and they're like, 'Oh, can you send me that one'.

ISABELLA: You're, like, the centre of naked photos in your group, I don't know.

SARAH: A lot of times that it happened in high school, guys would be in a group together texting.

ISABELLA: Yeah and they send it to their friend, like a random, and then their friend...

ASHLEY: I've got a 17-year-old brother and him and his friends will be there and I'll say 'What are you looking at?', and they're like 'Nothing!'. Yeah, they always do it in a little group.

Gathering, showing and distributing nude images of girls and women was recognised as a method by which boys and men can accumulate status and respect amongst their peers. This can encourage predatory behaviour as boys and men solicited pictures from girls and women with the promise of keeping them private while intending to 'collect' and show them to others. Kath suggested that teenaged boys might be motivated to gather and show 'nudes' of girls to other boys in order to establish their popularity and heterosexual appeal:

> I think there's pressure. I think especially if you're younger, if a boy can get ten pics of topless girls then he's going to be popular, he'll be cool or whatever, and I think there's some pressure there.

Young people felt that boys might also feel this 'pressure' once in a stable dating relationship. Displaying the attractiveness of a female partner and proving that she is infatuated enough to provide him with an image are reasons why a boy might show a 'private' image of his partner to others. Participants in one focus group described the probable motives of the boy, such as:

NATALIE: Look how hot my girlfriend is.
ALAN: Popularity, attention.
LEILA: Yeah, I think it's popularity that a girl actually sent him a photo of herself.

The production of male 'pride' through the non-consensual circulation of 'nudes' was particularly likely in the aftermath of a break-up. This is one of the most common scenarios in which non-consensual 'sexting' comes to the attention of the police (Salter et al., 2013). Hurt and humiliated when a relationship ends, a boy or man might publish a 'private' image of his ex-partner in revenge. This act is often attended by claims that the female partner had been unfaithful and hence 'deserves' to be publicly exposed as a 'slut'. Mark said:

> I've seen on Facebook and stuff, people have been cheated on or whatever for a couple of months and the boyfriend's found out and they've put it online as like a retaliation kind of thing.

There is, of course, no justification for non-consensually circulating a private image of a partner or ex-partner. Claims from the male partner that the female ex-partner is deserving of retribution for leaving him are frequently attended by allegations of infidelity (Vandello and Cohen, 2003). Violence during and following separation is a way that men attempt to restore feelings of lost pride and honour, not only in their own minds but also amongst their peers (Hearn and Whitehead, 2006). Online abuse appears to function in a similar fashion for boys and men, constituting a particularly public assertion of power against an ex-partner. Hope's report was typical:

> It was a girl in my school, when we were in Year 9, she had a photo of herself in a very gratuitous position, and she sent it to the boyfriend and they broke up and he sent it to everyone in our year. It went viral, and she ended up leaving the school.

In such cases, online abuse can be understood as an attempt not only to enact 'revenge' on the female partner but arguably as a way of restoring lost masculine status in the aftermath of a brea-kup. When explaining why boys and men share images with others, Chris said:

> Well, he sent it to his mate so it's a sense of pride. That's what I said before, in the society we live in, it's sort of that women are seen as different to men in the sexual aspect when it comes to things like this. So women are victimised, where men see it as pride.

Whether the image is of a current or ex-partner, acquaintance or stranger, a 'nude' could be exchanged with other boys and men in return for social recognition. Ringrose and colleagues (2013) provide a detailed examination of young people's practices of image exchange in high school, suggesting that collecting and showing nude images of girls is a way that boys could display their sexual proficiency to other boys (see also Harvey and Ringrose, 2015). The derogation of the girl or woman depicted is not incidental or external to this exchange but an important aspect of it. Online abuse involves a display of power and an act of moral transgression that, by affirming the power differential between perpetrator and victim, staked a claim in wider peer hierarchies. In the following excerpt, a woman in the focus group asks a man a follow-up question about a sexting incident:

AYLA: Remember that story you were telling us about the popular girl who got photos sent around and how she got teased for a couple of months. I was wondering if anything happened to the guy who sent them, did anyone tease him about it?

ADAM: No, he was [seen as] a champion and that sort of thing.

AYLA: So guys get praised for like…

ADAM: No, it depends on who you are. If it was me that sent it in high school I'd probably have the shit kicked out of me by someone. But because this guy was also up there, nothing happened to him, it was just like 'oh yeah, sick, man'.

AYLA: It's like everything else at high school, the hierarchy.

In this incident, both the perpetrator and the victim were considered 'up there' or popular in the school's peer hierarchy. By victimising a girl of equivalent status, the boy was a 'champion': he had displayed his sexual prowess and callous disregard for the wellbeing of the girl, and thus publicly affirmed the dominance of boys over girls in their peer group. However, Adam suggests that an equivalent act of perpetration committed by lower status boy would have been understood very differently. A lower status boy victimising a higher status girl would, Adam surmised, have invited retaliation from the higher status boys in order to reaffirm the stratification of the peer hierarchy. 'Nudes' were clearly potent objects in the peer contexts of young people and could be put to a range of uses by boys and men in their negotiations of status and performances of masculinity, motivating serious breaches of trust and invasions of privacy in order to shore up masculine status and affirm it in the eyes of others.

'Nudes' were clearly potent objects in the peer contexts of young people and could be put to a range of uses. They were highly sought after by boys and men, and young women found themselves being routinely asked to provide such images. In the following extended discussion, young women discuss their response to constant requests for nude images from friends and strangers.

LANA: I remember when I broke up with my boyfriend, all these guys I hardly spoke to were like 'Oh, send me a picture'. I'm like 'Who are you?' It's really awkward, a lot of boys ask for photos.

FACILITATOR: How do they ask?

LANA: They just ask.

SARAH: [They say] 'Send me a pic'.

WENDY: They text, like sexting.

MARIA: Yeah, 'Will you send a pic'.

LANA: Then you awkwardly have to stop talking to them.

FACILITATOR: Who's been asked?

ASHLEY: Yeah, I have.

FACILITATOR: And you guys have never been asked? [Men in the room shake their heads]

FACILITATOR: And if you don't want to send the text or the sext, what happens?

ISABELLA: You just ignore them.

JAYLEE: You just go like, 'I'm going to bed now. Bye'.

ASHLEY: I'm not one of these people who are like 'No, screw you, who are you?' because I feel mean.

JAYLEE: Me too. I just try to avoid the situation.

SARAH: It depends on who the person is. If it's someone that you're actually friends with, I'd say, 'This is really awkward, don't know how to respond to that', but if it's someone else, I don't care.

ASHLEY: Yeah, actually…

FACILITATOR: So male friends have asked?

LANA: Yeah, and then they pretend it's a joke when you reject them.

MARIA: Yeah.

LANA: They go 'Oh, I was just joking'.

JAYLEE: And sometimes they'll be like 'I'll send you one if you send me one'. I'm like 'I'm not interested, I don't want to see your naked photo'.

REECE: This is fascinating.

Young women felt challenged articulating sexual non-consent and refusal in a cultural context where femininity continues to be constructed around norms of affability and agreeability. Just saying 'no' would, as Ashley said, 'feel mean'. Nonetheless, young women developed strategies in order to extricate themselves from friendships and circumstances characterised by unwanted pressure to provide nude images. Rather than saying 'no', one young woman said 'you awkwardly have to stop talking to them' and another suggested 'I just try to avoid the situation'. Nonetheless, these requests clearly had a negative impact on young women's view of the man who made them.

FACILITATOR: So how does it change a friendship, like with the guy, once you've gotten that request [for a nude], do you just pretend it just never happened?

ISABELLA: It depends how close you are with them. It depends if you want that friendship, if you want to keep it, or if you're just like 'No, screw you'.

SARAH: It changes my view on the person.

LANA: I wouldn't lose a friendship over someone asking me. A lot of my really close friends are all guys and I know what they're like. I spend a lot of time with them and they talk to me about stuff that I'm like 'Okay, just go in the other room and talk about it, I don't want to know'. So I guess that's just them. So if they asked it to me [for a nude], and I was like 'No, go away', I would just be [she shrugs] because I know that's just what they're like.

SARAH: That's the thing, it depends on who the person is and what kind of relationship you have, it totally comes down to that.

In this discussion, Sarah emphasised that a request for a 'nude' 'changes my view' of the boy or man, while agreeing with Isabella that she would weigh up the importance of the friendship in her response. However, for Lana, it's up to the girl to take these requests in her stride. She suggests 'that's just what they're [boys] like'. Male sexual pressure is understood as an inevitable feature of male–female friendships that girls and women must accept and manage. This may include an abrupt 'no, go away' but Lana describes this response as purely hypothetical, and what she might do 'if they asked it to me'. In practice, it seemed that young women found the outright rejection of male requests for 'nudes' more difficult to assert.

On the whole, young women abstained from any firm judgement or moral assessment of the boys and men who placed them in this position. Instead, they adopted a high degree of responsibility to, first, shield the boy or man from any knowledge that his request had made them uncomfortable, and, second, to manage the risk of abuse within the relationship (by stopping talking to them or avoiding them). The possibility of saying 'no, screw you' was discussed but did not seem to find purchase in their lived experience, which involved avoiding any outright confrontation. This internalisation of responsibility, and the corresponding exculpation of male wrongdoing, was reproduced in young people's discussions of the apparently ubiquitous 'dick pic'.

The 'dick pic'

Multiple female participants in this study described receiving unsolicited photos of male genitals (known colloquially as 'dick pics') from male acquaintances and friends. Much like requests for 'nudes', this put them in an uncomfortable situation. On the whole, young women felt uncertain about how to respond, or the motivations behind the image. Suspicion of female culpability in their own victimisation was pervasive enough to put women on the defensive for simply receiving an unwanted 'dick pic'. In the following excerpt, Isabella describes being sent a video and photo of a man's erection after meeting him only briefly.

ISABELLA: Like, I was friends with the kid that was like his best friend, and then, like, one time I met him, so it was, like, all right, whatever. And then we spoke for that one time and that was it, and then he sent me Snapchats before but it was just like normal [not sexual], but then I saw the video and the photo [of his penis] and I was like 'Nah, that's weird'. And then yeah, that's how it like eventuated.

ZANE: Yeah, right, 'cause don't you have to like accept him before…

ISABELLA: Yes. I knew him. I know him. Like, we've spoken. Like…

SARAH: But it's not like you were really close.

ISABELLA: No, I know. I just don't know how to like explain how I know him. Like, it's not like he was a stranger and I was like 'oh yeah'.

In this excerpt, Isabella went to some lengths to distance herself from any suggestion that she was, in some way, responsible for receiving this unwanted image and video. She emphasised the tenuous connection between her and the boy, the fact that they'd only met once, her disinterest in him (he was 'whatever') and their infrequent contact. Despite these qualifications, Zane interjects that she could only receive Snapchats from him if she had 'accepted' him online. She immediately rejects the inference that this might render her culpable for the 'dick pic', and is supported by Sarah ('it's not like you were really close'). Isabella felt that the onus was on her to establish that she was not responsible for his conduct, and becomes frustrated trying to explain that she 'knows' him but not in a way that excused his behaviour. She was exasperated trying to explain his behaviour or the expected response from her:

> Yeah I don't know why they do it. What was he expecting, I have never replied to any Snapchats ever, and what are you meant to say back? 'Oh, you really look good there.' What am I meant to do?

The ubiquity of the 'dick pic' prompted prolonged discussions in focus groups about the nature of male sexuality. On the whole, young women shared Isabella's bewilderment about why boys and men were sending these images and what they expected in return. The 'dick pic' was often explained as a kind of misunderstanding, in which boys and men were sending an image in an attempt to solicit an image in return from the girl. Sarah adds:

> Maybe it's reciprocal, because the guys they want to see the girls' genitals, so then they think, 'Oh so if I'm a girl I want to see the opposite sex's genitals'. But that's a really simple way of thinking.

Attempts to explain the 'dick pic' as a friendly invitation to sexual communication foundered as young women observed that 'dick pics' were often sent with aggressive and harassing overtones, such as when boys and men send multiple unwanted images in the early hours of the morning. Nonetheless, young women generally avoided attributing a harassing motivation to purveyors of 'dick pics'. Instead, they turned to essentialist notions of male sexuality as 'more visual', genitally focused and uncontrollable, in comparison to female sexuality which was understood as more holistic and incorporating the whole person.

LAUREN: I don't think girls are that interested in getting images from guys, as guys are from girls.

NANCY: Guys are more visual.

LAUREN: Yeah.

NADINE: But like yeah girls would generally never ask for – oh well maybe, but it would be less.

STEPHEN: There are girls out there who will.

NADINE: Yeah for sure, but in comparison to the guys. I was going to say, if it's like [a picture of] a guy topless, that would be something they [girls] would more likely receive than everything [a nude image] and want to see everything. Well, certainly I don't want to see everything.

The sending of 'dick pics' was typically explained through discourses of polarised and essentialist gender differences. Male sexual wrongdoing was likely to be excused as a mistake driven by uncontrollable sexual drives in contrast to female sexuality, which was governed by a capacity for choice and agency not attributed to masculinity. While this constituted female sexuality as an active and autonomous force, this was accomplished through an exculpation of male responsibility and the positioning of girls and women as the ultimate arbiters of sexual morality. This represents a new iteration of the traditional role of women as 'God's police' (Summers, 1975) and responsible for upholding moral standards in the face of male animality or avarice. This has the effect of obscuring the harassing and coercive dimensions of online abuse since male sexual aggression can be positioned as an inadvertent 'mistake' or just an inevitable fact of life for some 'unlucky' girl.

LANA: Sometimes I think you've just got to be really unlucky. Like one of my really good friends, she was being sent images from a guy who had a girlfriend, but I don't know what his motivation was. He kept sending her stuff that was pretty explicit. She wouldn't give anything in return, but he was, and like, she didn't do anything about it, she didn't tell his girlfriend. She told me but I haven't told anyone, like you sort of need to be unlucky. Some people, they would definitely be telling people and then it sucks to be the person who made the mistake.

FACILITATOR: How did your friend feel to just get sent random images of...

LANA: Oh, well, they were like good friends, but he just kind of pushed it too far, she didn't really want to see that [a nude image]. Well she – I don't know if she kept them or deleted them. I think she deleted some. But yeah, she was just really confused, like she was like 'is that like cheating'? I don't know, I don't think she was fully violated, but she – yeah I guess was confused 'cause he had a girlfriend.

Despite recognising her friend's discomfort at this unwanted explicit communication, Lana resisted any attribution of responsibility to the boy in this scenario. She questions whether her friend had been 'fully violated' and suggests instead that she was simply 'unlucky'. She emphasised that the boy had potentially put himself at risk of humiliation or the end of his relationship if his 'dick pic' was made known to others, but this was understood as a 'mistake' or misunderstanding on his behalf – 'he just kind of pushed it too far'. While her friend was simply 'unlucky' to receive these images, Lana also argued that girls who are victimised by the non-consensual circulation of private images 'sort of bring it upon themselves, like in sending it in the first place'. This reluctance to attribute culpability to boys and men for online abuse was common in focus groups, where young women often spoke of their discomfort and distress at receiving unwanted images but did not hold the sender responsible for his actions. Interestingly, on the rare occasions that 'dick pics' were identified as sexual harassment, it was young men rather than young women speaking. Ray said, 'I've got a bunch of female friends who've got pictures of guys' cocks, just randomly [sent to them]. So I mean that – I can compare that to the flasher with the raincoat really.'

Online abuse, responsibility and justice

While young people recognised gendered power imbalances at the level of relationships and on social media, the locus of control, and therefore responsibility, was consistently located in girls and women. Even where young people recognised that girls and women experience pressure to provide images to boys, they could be blamed for simply feeling this pressure in the first place. For example, in the exchange below, Rod rejects the notion that girls experience 'cultural' pressure to send boys 'nudes', emphasising that this 'pressure' arises within individual girls.

ROD: I think the pressure is inner-built pressure, if a girl's going to want to send a photo she's going to do it because she feels he really wants it, like she wants to be liked by him or approved by him, almost looking for his satisfaction. I don't know how to put it, I don't think it's necessarily a cultural thing, it's more like individual pressure.

ALICIA: To make sure the boyfriend's happy so he stays with you.

ROD: That kind of pressure.

This individualising discourse emphasised the responsibility of girls and young women for their sexual choices while downplaying the contribution of contextual or relational factors, or the role of male wrongdoing. This was linked to a notion of gender equality in which acknowledging victimisation in online abuse was considered patronising to girls and women and 'unfair' to boys and men. When discussing an incident mentioned in the news media in which a 17-year-old boy non-consensually circulated a still image of himself and his ex-partner taken from a sexual video they had made during the relationship, Alicia complained that the prosecution of the boy was overly harsh and an 'unfair balance of responsibility':

ALICIA: [S]houldn't she have taken some responsibility at the same time for taking that action, knowing that he could have done anything with it? So, I don't know, I think there's an unfair balance of responsibility here, that because he's the guy and she's vulnerable – I'm not saying she's not vulnerable, I'm saying there's this betrayal, that because she's the woman, she's the one that needs to be taken care of, whereas he's the one that needs to be punished.

ROD: So you think if she was the one who sent the picture she wouldn't be charged?

ALICIA: Not as severely at all.

Alicia recognised that the girl depicted in the image was 'vulnerable', but she was more concerned about what she sees as the 'betrayal' of the boy. She suggested that the girl in the incident is being treated as 'the one that needs to be taken care of', not because she's been genuinely harmed, but primarily 'because she's the woman', whereas the boy is being 'punished' because 'he's the guy'. In response to Rod's question, she insists that, if the roles were reversed, the woman wouldn't be charged 'as severely at all'. In this exchange, Alicia assumes that intervention of the criminal justice system in favour of the woman, who is not being forced to accept 'responsibility' and face humiliation for consenting to make the image in the first place. In her view, 'fairness' requires the criminal justice system to treat the male perpetrator and female victim as the 'same', rather than to enforce the law or punish wrongdoing.

This is a position that implicitly, as McRobbie (2004) put it, 'takes feminism into account' by acknowledging feminist concerns about gender inequality but folding them into a framework that consigns feminism to history. Gender equality is then conflated with gender neutrality and the demand that men and women are treated the 'same'. Alicia objects to the punishing of the male perpetrator because she feels that it denies the responsibility of the female victim, thus infantilising her as someone who 'needs to be taken care of'. The ostensibly feminist sentiment of female autonomy is thus married to the blaming of victims of online abuse. Discussing the victim in this incident, Eloise noted 'it doesn't speak very highly of her character, she made the sex tape' and questioned her decisions to go to the police. This is a discourse in which online abuse is not something to be punished, but rather the abuse itself operates as a justifiable punishment of the girl for breaching gender norms. The intervention of the criminal justice system into online abuse is thus as an external interference in a necessary process: the shaming of the girl for breaching appropriate feminine behaviour.

When discussing online abuse, young people rarely referred to the police or the justice system as potential arbiters. As evidenced in Alicia's quote, this may have been because online abuse was understood by some participants as an informal but appropriate way of 'policing' girls and women. However, young people were also uncertain whether the intervention of the criminal justice system would do more good than harm. Steph voiced her concerns about the potentially disproportionate legal responses to young people or minors who are non-consensually circulating images of others. She noted that they might end up with a conviction for a sex offence with serious and disproportionate consequences:

> [B]ecause a lot of the kids are so young that are involved, I think it would be really harsh for them to not get a job or you know, not be allowed to work with kids because of a stupid decision they made. I think that's really unfair because they're usually just – it's just a dumb mistake they make. But yeah, I definitely think police should take action, but not have them have this record, but just to – yeah, I guess, it's the most effective I think when the kids are warned from a young age that this isn't a good behaviour and it can be destructive and dangerous and they should know about that.

Young people argued for nuanced legal responses to online abuse that recognised the diminished responsibility of minors, did not criminalise consensual image production but only non-consensual distribution, and made allowances for the different motives and impacts of online abuse. In their own lives and experiences, legal redress was the option of last resort, and they generally expected themselves and their peers to manage the risks and impacts of online abuse amongst themselves. This was shaped by a highly individualistic vocabulary of choice and responsibility that disproportionately burdened girls and women with the work of managing risk on social media, and effaced the role of boys and men as perpetrators or complicit bystanders. Without that individualising narrative, young people could struggle to 'make meaning' out of online abuse in a way that didn't ascribe a hopeless position to girls and women. In the following excerpt, Matilda brought up an incident in which a young woman was filmed having sex with a male sports star and the video was distributed online. While the man was deemed to have gotten off 'scott free', the woman in the scenario was described as being 'punished for life':

MATILDA: But that has to be with the double standard as well, because that video I was talking about, about the boy and the girl and the toilets having sex and the video got distributed, the girl was really seen as a whore, and she was made fun of everywhere throughout the country, but you never heard the guy. The girl had no life after that, but the guy was cool that he did that.

STEPH: He got off scot free.

MATILDA: Yeah exactly, and the girl was punished for life.

JOANNA: That's always the case, the guys come out as legends and the girls are a slut. There's no winning for girls essentially.

ALAN: Yeah you're either a prude or a slut.

JOANNA: Yeah, you can't win, it's a very fine line.

If it's 'always' the case that men are 'legends' and women are 'sluts' in online abuse, Joanna felt there was 'no winning for girls'; that is, there were no practical steps that girls and women can take to change the situation or make progress against online abuse. Discourses of individual responsibility (often underpinned by essentialist notions of gender difference) left young people feeling hopeless – 'you can't win' – if the 'cultural scaffolding' (Gavey, 2005) of online abuse cannot be surmounted by individual effort or resistance. However, as they recounted their experiences of online abuse, a number of scenarios emerged in focus groups in which young people described moments of conflict and change in online abuse and the underlying gendered inequalities. The next section discusses four such examples: a) bystander intervention, b) bystander de-escalation, c) counter-circulation, and d) subversion.

a) Bystander intervention

As previously discussed, boys at school often collected 'nudes' to display to each other. This was a source of tension within peer groups characterised by platonic as well as romantic relationships between boys and girls. Girls resented the sharing and exchange of these images in social settings, which boys generally attempted to keep secret from female friends out of embarrassment. Rachel said:

You would be at a party and then you'd see a group of people just assembled very closely together, mostly guys, and you'd be like 'What are you doing', and they were like 'Oh nothing', because they would be ashamed of it in front of us girls. But it turns out that one of them had an ex-girlfriend that used to go to our school and he still had these residual pictures. So it was just this sort of grandstanding thing, 'I still have the pictures and you know, look at what I got' sort of thing.

Young women described their disappointment and anger when they were confronted with evidence of male friends bonding by showing 'nudes' to one another. Donna recalled challenging a group of male friends as they crowded around the 'nudes' on a boy's phone: 'They're like "Look at this, look at this", and I was like "Are you guys seriously just looking at this right now?".' Young women particularly objected when 'nudes' were being shown in front of them, which they interpreted as a show of disrespect towards themselves and other girls present, and potentially towards the girl depicted in the image. Jaylee described an incident in which her friend found that her male 'best friend' had a 'nude' of her on his phone:

I was sitting with this group of guys and I look over and there was a photo of a girl, and I was sitting next to my friend and she was like, 'Grab that phone', and she grabbed it and she realised it was her. So that's when it gets awkward, and then she full had a go at it because she's like 'You're my best mate, what are you doing', and he's like 'I didn't even know it was you'. So it's so weird.

A preferred discourse of gender neutrality required girls and women to maintain a 'schizoid' (Renold and Ringrose, 2011) semi-awareness of the potential for gendered abuse while formally disavowing knowledge of, or rationalising away, any such risks in their own lives and peer contexts. This delicate balance of knowing-but-not-knowing was destabilised in the incidents described by Rachel and Jaylee, in which girls were confronted with the close proximity of online abuse and its perpetration by male friends and acquaintances. This could trigger accusations from girls and women (as Jaylee said about her friend, 'she full had a go at it') that their male friends were acting in hypocritical and exploitative ways; the kinds of direct expressions of disagreement that they typically avoided when solicited for 'nudes' or sent 'dick pics'. It was clear that both young men and women valued their platonic friendships with each other and these were at stake when boys and men engaged in online abuse, generating moments of conflict in which the girls and women demanded the enactment of gender equality in deed as well as word.

b) Bystander de-escalation

Young men in the focus groups expressed concern about the impacts of online abuse on girls and women, and agreed that the humiliation of girls through the circulation of 'nudes' and 'dick pics' was unfair. This concern could be enacted in ways that disrupted online abuse. In the following exert, Huan described an incident in high school in which his group of friends came across a lost phone. It belonged to a male classmate and contained an image of a girl that had been 'sent around'. As Huan says below, the boys 'quite liked the person' in the image and agreed 'don't show anyone'.

HUAN: Well one of my mates a couple of years ago found a phone, someone's phone – left in class. I can't remember exactly, but it had photos of obviously received messages, it had photos of – like this was before Snapchat actually – but this person just sent a photograph. They found on this, you know, like a pretty popular attractive girl in my grade, she'd obviously sent them to this phone and he sort of passed it around to a bunch of his mates and stuff. It didn't sort of go – nothing really happened though, but it was sort of – it was mainly just a small group of guys that it went around to. No-one sort of sent it out en masse…

FACILITATOR: Okay so it was kind of contained, it got sent around but it didn't kind of…

HUAN: It was mostly just around a group of friends who sent it around, that he sent it around to.

FACILITATOR: And just no-one put it on Facebook or Twitter.

HUAN: No, apparently everyone decided that it would be going too far; showed remarkable restraint actually.

SEBASTIAN: With my one [an incident of online abuse] I remember they made a fake account with her name and put that picture [her nude] as her profile picture. Then it got deleted off Facebook.

FACILITATOR: So that's interesting, so your friends, I mean did you guys sort of talk about it?

HUAN: I wasn't that involved with it, but it was – I think they must have talked about it and said don't show anyone. I think they actually did quite like the person and it was a bit of a shock kind of thing.

This incident demonstrates the key role that bystanders can play in de-escalating or defusing online abuse. The boys accidentally found a phone containing a 'nude' and, potentially, they could have capitalised on the find by circulating the image more broadly. Huan recalled that his friends viewed the girl in the image as a friend, 'it was a bit of a shock' that she'd made the image in the first place, and showed 'remarkable restraint' in not showing the image to anyone else. She had already been embarrassed by the circulation of the image and they didn't want to add to this. The nature of social media is such that online abuse necessarily requires others to participate in the abuse by, in this case, 'forwarding' on intimate images. In contrast, refusal to participate necessarily short-circuits the abuse and protects the victim from further harm.

c) Counter-circulation

Much of the impunity to humiliation enjoyed by boys and men in online publics is premised on the expected nature of public masculinity, up to and including vulgar bodily display. There was some evidence in focus groups that the taken-for-granted qualities of the public male body were being eroded online. As the discussion of 'gym selfies' suggests, the male body can be incorporated into masculine 'identity projects' to be modified and displayed in the achievement of an idealised masculinity (Patterson and Elliott, 2002). Masculinity is becoming an increasingly visual accomplishment shaped by idealised depictions of muscular physicality in consumer culture (Gill et al., 2005). This trend has been arguably exacerbated by the increased availability of pornography online (Cook, 2005). The excerpt below suggests that the objectification of the male form, and it's assessment against the standards set by advertising and pornography, may be generating opportunities for retaliation against online abuse.

Reece described what happened when a male friend at high school sent a 'dick pic' and it was circulated to others. In focus groups, the prevailing assumption was that boys and men could send 'dick pics' without fear of retaliation because girls and women were disinclined to circulate them to others, and if they did, male nudity had few consequences for boys and men. In this case the boy was vulnerable to collective humiliation because he was thought to have a small penis, or a 'peanut'. Rather than acting as a sexual advance or assertion of power, his 'dick pic' instead became a humiliating public testament to his perceived masculine inadequacies. Reece said:

REECE: There was a guy, some of my friends, yeah, he sent a picture to his girlfriend or something and it got around, and he wasn't very well… ah endowed, very well equipped down there. And it went around and people were like 'I don't even know why we all want to see this'.
ISABELLA: It was to a random girl?
REECE: He sent it to a few girls I think… Everyone was pretty cruel to him about it, they called him peanut for ages, and sometimes we still do call him peanut. It's kind of just become like a thing now. But yeah, we were pretty cruel to him about it. Like he could have gone and done something bad, like committed suicide about it, because we were pretty harsh about it.

There is some ambiguity about precisely who this image was sent to, since Reece nominates 'his girlfriend or something' and then 'a few girls I think'. It could potentially be a case of non-consensual 'sexting' if it was circulated by his girlfriend at the time; however, Reece qualifies this somewhat, suggesting there were multiple recipients. It is telling that this was the only incident recounted in all the focus groups in which a boy faced judgement or criticism for sending a 'dick pic'. This indicates the rarity of such criticism, but it also suggests that the relative impunity to embarrassment enjoyed by boys and men in online publics is not fixed but rather it remains a site of contestation.

By demonstrating to boys and men that online abuse can have consequences for them, the threat of counter-circulation may potentially inhibit this form of sexual harassment. As a response to online abuse, however, counter-circulation is legally problematic and ethically ambiguous at best. If the boy in the incident recounted by Reece was under the age of 16, then the girl who circulated the image could have been culpable under child pornography statutes. A new raft of 'revenge porn' laws in a range of jurisdictions seeks to criminalise the non-consensual circulation of nude images more generally, particularly in the case of self-manufactured 'selfies' (as this image apparently was). Counter-circulation could risk serious legal consequences.

Furthermore, while there may be a certain 'poetic justice' to such incidents, counter-circulation does not ameliorate the harms of online abuse but rather adds to these harms through the deliberate humiliation of the sender.

d) Subversion

Social media can act as a forum for the emergence of spontaneous and unexpected responses to online abuse. In the following discussion, Sarah describes her friend using Snapchat to capture and distribute graphic images and video of the bodies that she sees on the UK medical television show Embarrassing Bodies. The show focuses on common but 'embarrassing' (often sexual) problems such as sexually transmitted infections, and genitals or breasts considered outside the ideal of consumer culture and pornography. As Sarah described her friend taking and distributing these images, it emerged that Ashley and Jaylee were also taking photos and videos of the show.

SARAH: My friend uses Snapchat like it's a Bible. She's addicted to Snapchat. Every second I'm like 'What are you doing?' The other night we watched Embarrassing Bodies – that's an interesting show. Have you guys ever seen that?... She takes videos of the show and sends it to all her contacts on Snapchat... 'Cause it'll come up and it'll be like a really nasty something.

ASHLEY: That's kind of counted as sexting.

SARAH: Like some people use it [Snapchat] all the time.

FACILITATOR: What's the show, it's called...?

SARAH: Embarrassing Bodies.

FACILITATOR: Okay, so it's a show and it's about people with bad bodies who go...?

ISABELLA: No, [it's for] things [bodies] that are wrong. This man that was on there the other day had a brain tumour and it made him produce breast milk, that's why he went on so he could stop producing breast milk and get rid of the brain tumour.

FACILITATOR: And they get medical treatment?

ASHLEY: Yeah but it's on this show.

NADIRA: But usually it's people with like genital kind of things. And they'll just show you…

SARAH: And there's no filter, it just shows everything.

ASHLEY: Yeah, and most of it's like vomit worthy.

SARAH: Yeah, it's pretty gross.

FACILITATOR: So your friend then takes photos of…

SARAH: She'll like do videos.

ASHLEY: I have one on my phone.

SARAH: It's like a weekly thing now and we watch it.

JAYLEE: Yeah, like 'cause this girl, she had something wrong with her boobs and she put her hands up and her underarms were hairy as. It was like, 'You have a bigger problem under your arms'. So I took a heap of photos.

This exchange was marked by raucous laughter throughout. As a social media platform, Snapchat rose to prominence because of its potential utility in 'sexting', since it promises that all images sent on the app will be automatically erased. Images of hairy armpits and sexually transmitted infections are the precise inversion of the 'nudes' and 'dick pics' that these young women had previously been discussing their response to. The proposition that a young woman might respond to a Snapchat request for a 'nude' with an image of a sexually transmitted infection or hairy underarms prompted much hilarity. This method is unlikely to catalyse much change in the abusive practices of men and boys, but at least it provided a humorous way of dispelling the discomfort and tension generated by incessant demands for 'nudes' and the receipt of 'dick pics' on the app.

Conclusion

Online abuse is often trivialised as just 'mean words on the internet' but this chapter has emphasised how the content of online abuse is inextricably linked to patterns of harassing and intrusive conduct, embedded within larger inequalities of power. In the manufacture and exchange of intimate images, a gendered double standard enabled images of female and male bodies to be 'weaponised' in different ways. Images of female bodies were, for some boys and young men, potent symbols of their heterosexual prowess, and could be collected and displayed in derogatory ways as affirmations of masculine status. While images of female bodies circulated in ways that belittled or humiliated girls and women, images of male bodies – specifically, male genitals – also circulated in ways that negatively impacted on girls and women. Young women reported discomfort and uncertainty about the frequency with which they were being sent unwanted 'dick pics', which had the effect of introducing a coercive sexualised dimension into relations with male friends and acquaintances. The online visual economy thus pervasively disadvantaged girls and women in comparison to boys and men. In young people's experiences, these inequalities were disavowed within a ubiquitous language of individual choice and responsibility that tended to disavow the masculinity of online abuse perpetration. Whether it involved the non-consensual sending or receiving of 'nudes', the locus of control in online abuse was a feminine one; men and boys were largely excused. Instead, young people often defaulted to essentialist arguments that male sexual wrongdoing is inevitable or so expected it didn't constitute 'wrongdoing' in any meaningful sense. Nonetheless, they articulated a number of moments of breach or disruption in the gendered logics of online abuse, which foregrounds the importance of providing young people with alternative ways of responding to and intervening in online abuse. This point is taken up further in the Conclusion in this book.

Suggested links

The Line is an Australian campaign that aims to prevent abuse and violence and promote healthy and respectful relationships. The website contains advice to teenagers about how to manage and respond to pressure to provide 'nudes': www.theline.org.au/send-me-a-sext.

After two high-profile incidents in which 'dick pics' were circulated without the consent of the men depicted, *Guardian* columnist Jessica Valenti (Twitter:

@JessicaValenti) emphasised that men are also victims of 'revenge porn' in this 2014 article: www.theguardian.com/commentisfree/2014/jun/26/revenge-porn-victim-conservative-man-penis.

Journalist Clem Bastow describes the overlap between digital abuse and domestic violence: www.dailylife.com.au/news-and-views/news-features/digital-abuse-is-the-new-frontier-of-domestic-violence-20140216-32tsu.html.

6

FROM #OPGABON TO #OPDEATHEATERS

Transnational justice flows on social media

Social media offers an array of communicative opportunities associated with novel discourses and understandings of crime and justice. The exponentially expanded number of interlocutors and the increasingly porous boundaries between social media and the mass media provides multiple pathways to publicity, and new opportunities to debate and conceptualise social problems. This is key to the appeal of social media for social movements and activists. As Benhabib (1992: 79) observed, 'The struggle over what gets included in the public agenda is itself a struggle for justice and freedom.' It is not that social problems enter into the public domain fully formed but, rather, once they are on the 'public agenda', they become accessible to 'debate, reflection, action, and moral-political transformation' (Benhabib, 1992: 94). However, the 'filtering effects of the bourgeois public sphere', such as those hegemonic tendencies described in Chapter 2, can prevent some forms of suffering from reaching the 'level of political thematization and organization' (Fraser and Honneth, 2003: 116). These social problems remain, in effect, 'privatised'; refused symbolisation in the public sphere, consigning affected individuals or groups to the doubled injury of ongoing suffering and the denial of that suffering. On social media, suppressed individual or social struggles can find articulation, and potential responses can be debated. Social media has also provided mechanisms whereby new formulations of justice can be enacted, such as when women use social media to 'name and shame' perpetrators of sexual violence (Salter, 2013a). Such practices can be critiqued as vigilantism and a form of 'trial by media' (Greer and McLaughlin, 2011) but they should be contextualised within the pervasive failings of the justice system and mass media to address the extent and impact of interpersonal victimisation both 'online' and 'offline'.

There are unanswered questions about the political efficacy of alternative discourses of crime and justice on social media. The ideal of deliberative democracy places the public sphere in a constructive but critical tension with the powers of a nationally bounded government. The public sphere is understood to be functioning in the interests of democracy by independently scrutinising the government and other authorities, and developing shared understandings and points of consensus which are incorporated into democratic decision-making through elections and other mechanisms (McKee, 2004). This is sometimes described as the communicative flow from the 'weak publics' of the media and other public deliberative fora to the 'strong publics', primarily the parliament of a nation state, with the sovereign power to act on public opinion (Fraser, 1990). Social media appears to operate outside the ideal of deliberative democracy in ways that challenge optimistic assessments of its potential as a tool for social change or transformation. It is true that social media is relatively inclusive and diverse in comparison to established media industries such as newspapers, television and radio, whose exclusionary and mono-cultural tendencies have been a recurrent source of criticism. However, simply being inclusive does not make social media politically efficacious. As philosopher Nancy Fraser (2014: 9) has argued:

> publicity is supposed to hold officials accountable and to assure that the actions of the state express the will of the citizenry. Thus, a public sphere should correlate with a sovereign power.

She goes on to question the critical potential of the globalised public discourse enabled by new media technologies, which acts in effect as a 'weak public' whose shared understandings and discourses appear to lack any identifiable 'strong public' with the power to act on them. In his study of the political impacts of social media, Gerbaudo (2012) notes that one of the strengths of social media for social movements – its ability to generate networks of shared interest and affect between geographically dispersed actors – is also a significant risk. Social media has become 'particularly useful precisely because of the spatial dispersion characteristic of post-industrial society' (Gerbaudo, 2012: 34) but connections between users are often weak and ephemeral. This has the potential to disperse and dilute momentum towards collective action and exacerbate dynamics of exclusion and alienation. Core groups of dedicated activists, often although not necessarily geographically co-located, appear to be critical to realising the potential of social media for mobilisation and political activism, and in engaging more efficaciously with 'strong publics' with decision-making power (Bennett et al., 2009).

This chapter examines the question of the political efficacy of social media justice with reference to two interlinked initiatives by the activist network Anonymous. Anonymous's 2013 intervention in apparently politically connected ritual killings in the West African state of Gabon, called OpGabon (short for Operation Gabon), led to OpDeathEaters in 2014, a wide-ranging social media campaign against elite involvement in organised child abuse in the Global North as well as the Global South. In this process, Anonymous developed a complex critique of the role of elite deviance in international social and economic inequality that defied taken-for-granted distinctions between 'developed' and 'under-developed' countries. This chapter describes and analyses the emergence of OpDeathEaters from OpGabon as an example of the transnational circuits of public opinion emerging on social media that are producing new grammars of contestation and social protest. However, it asks whether mechanisms exist for the implementation of such novel forms of political consensus, emphasising the challenges of correlating transnational public opinion with mechanisms of public power.

The political efficacy of social media justice

As Chapter 1 describes, critical theory recognises that the underlying technological structures of the media contribute to the shape and form of public discourse and society more broadly. Habermas (1989) described how the invention of the printing press enabled the formation of a 'reading public' as 'private' letters and dispatches became publicly available newspapers and pamphlets. This 'reading public' had particular features that were determined by the characteristics of the print medium, including a relatively low cost of entry (printing presses were not particularly expensive) that facilitated a multitude of contributors and voices in the public sphere, although (as Chapter 2 noted) considerable social and economic barriers existed to the participation of women, the working class and other groups. The evolution of media technology has had a significant impact on the critical capacity and function of the public sphere. Habermas (1989) observed that the infrastructure of the mass media, such as television and cinema, is considerably more expensive than print and has centralised ownership in the hands of the state and the wealthy few. The inclusion of more diverse groups within the mass media as producers of content has proceeded at a slow pace, and subaltern groups frequently complain of negative and stereotypical representations in the mass media. The perception that mass media has lost its critical power and operates with, rather than at a distance from, established political and economic interests has contributed to a pervasive crisis of democratic legitimacy in many countries. Criminologists have persistently criticised the role of the mass media in sensationalising matters of crime and justice, often in ways that impact most severely on the disadvantaged and obscure entrenched inequalities (Greer and Reiner, 2012).

Since the 1970s, the emergence of networked computer technologies has provided a platform for moral discourses and related forms of political practice beyond the bounds of the mass mediated public sphere. This has included the facilitation and sponsorship of discourses and practices that directly contest the power of the state and seek to undermine the legal frameworks that delineate what and how information enters the public domain. In the United States in the early 1990s, for example, software developers released powerful free cryptographic software in breach of national security laws in protest against expanding government surveillance (Levy, 2001). Various streams of what might be called 'internet culture' have championed the values of file sharing and open source collaboration in direct contest to intellectual property, copyright and patent laws. The 'chan' boards described in Chapter 2 adhere to a radical interpretation of the right to free speech to the point of championing the sponsorship of hate speech and legitimising the distribution of child abuse material. Much of this activity has been informed by a macho libertarian culture dominant within hacking and engineering circles. The romanticisation of online counter-culturalism can overlook its misogynist strains, as well as its ideological affinities with right-wing free market individualism (Turner, 2010). Nonetheless, these examples illustrate how networked computing technologies such as the internet provide avenues for novel forms of political discussion and practice that have proven appealing to those alienated from more mainstream mechanisms of public participation and decision-making.

Social media has also enabled the formation and dissemination of counter-discourses to challenge the ways that allegations of crimes, and particularly sexual violence, have been publicly marginalised in the public sphere (Salter, 2013a). Research on the role of social media in justice-seeking has generally focused on the incorporation of social media into social movement politics, or the use of social media by individuals seeking recognition for specific wrongs (Dodge, 2016; Keller, 2012). The way in which social media might be reconfiguring notions of crime and justice more broadly has been overlooked, and so has Fraser's (2014) question about the political efficacy of online discourse and consensus. The low bar of entry to social media and the largely unregulated speech that it supports has facilitated a proliferation of claims of harm and injury of varying levels of persuasiveness. When a compelling case is made and finds sponsorship amongst other social media users, it's unclear how and where this consensus might be acted upon. In the absence of more formalised advocacy structures, such as community groups and non-government organisations, the translation of online discourse into political action is fraught. The much-debated fluidity of social media political movements, and their lack of a formal hierarchy, appears to prioritise inclusivity while sacrificing efficacy. What, then, is the role of social media in the public articulation of crime and justice, and what possibilities exist for the implementation of social media-sponsored political consensus? The following sections examine these issues by tracing the development of the social media 'operations' orchestrated under the imprimatur of Anonymous.

Anonymous

The term 'Anonymous' describes a loose collective that formed on the notorious image-board 4chan following its launch in 2003 (Coleman, 2014). They became known for enthusiastic and deliberately provocative campaigns of pranking and trolling that developed a more activist orientation in 2008, when 4chan targeted the Church of Scientology for its attempts to censor and suppress information critical of the Church. The scale of Anonymous's protests took the public by surprise, particularly when their online efforts (including various attacks on Scientology websites) were paired with substantive street rallies at multiple locations around the world (Coleman, 2014). This activist turn caused some consternation within 4chan which had been largely hostile to social movement politics (Dibbell, 2009). A split emerged within 4chan in 2010 as a considerable number of 'anons' mobilised in support of the whistleblower website Wikileaks, which had come under considerable international pressure after publishing voluminous secret diplomatic cables (Phillips, 2015: 148). Anonymous also actively supported the political uprisings in Tunisia, Egypt and Libya in 2011, triggering positive media coverage as well as an influx of new 4chan participants orientated towards political activism rather than pranks and 'lulz' (Phillips, 2015: 148). Anonymous's association with the Occupy Wall Street movement further cemented this political turn.

Phillips (2015: 151) suggests that there are now two largely separate groups claiming the Anonymous label: the first being a loose activist network with its origins in the various 'operations' from 2010, and the second being the 'anons' of 4chan. In the mass media and on social media, the term Anonymous is generally used to refer to the activist network, particularly as 4chan has become associated in public awareness with Gamergate and other less heroic 'operations'. In 2011, activists affiliated with Anonymous initiated OpGabon and, subsequently, OpDeathEaters, to bring international attention to bear on instances of the organised and sadistic sexual abuse of children. Organised sexual abuse has an unstable place in the public sphere, after an intensive period of denial during the 1990s in which children and adults who disclosed organised sexual abuse were routinely described by journalists as confabulators and fantasists (Salter, 2013b). The willingness of the mass media to entertain the possibility of organised sexual abuse has arguably expanded following the various clergy abuse scandals and the revelations that followed the death of UK entertainer Jimmy Savile, which the chapter will discuss shortly. However, recognition of organised sexual abuse remains uneven. A comparison between the two initiatives highlights the ways in which social media can sponsor the reformulation of understandings of crime and justice within a transnational frame, and publicly circulate these understandings on a scale that previous networked technologies could not.

OpGabon

Gabon or the Gabonese republic is a state on the west coast of Central Africa with an estimated population of 1.5 million. Since gaining independence from France in 1960, Gabon has had only three presidents. In 1967, Omar Bongo Ondimba became president following the death of his predecessor and declared Gabon a one-party state. He remained president for 41 years until his death in 2009, whereupon his son and current president Ali Bongo was elected to replace him. Since the 1990s, various democratic reforms and shows of political liberalisation have been countered by the centralisation of strong powers within the figure of the president. Although natural reserves have made Gabon one of the most prosperous countries in the region, income distribution is skewed towards the politically connected wealthy elite. The Bongo family has been accused of pocketing up to one-quarter of Gabon's gross domestic product in recent years. Despite allegations of corruption and nepotism, and the suppression of the press and interference in elections, the Bongo government enjoys good relations with the United States and the international community. The United States is a major importer of Gabon's crude oil. From 2011 to 2012, Gabon sat on the United Nations Security Council where it helped pass major American initiatives including sanctions against Iran's nuclear programme and support for the removal of Muammar Gaddafi in Libya.

Like other Sub-Saharan African countries, Gabon has a black market in human organs trafficked for use in rituals and the making of talismans that are supposed to imbue the owner with social influence and political power. This black market has its roots in what historian Florence

Bernault (2013: 176) calls 'the long tradition of making charms and medicine from human substances' in Gabon. In the nineteenth century, charms were made from the bones of relatives who died from natural causes, although human sacrifice was practiced in exceptional circumstances (Bernault, 2013: 178). These practices were transformed at the advent of French colonialism and the collapse of traditional economic, social and religious structures. Clandestine groups and networks of men in Gabon turned to ritual murder and charm-making in an effort to reclaim power and social standing (Bernault, 2013). A reported increase in ritual murders in Gabon since 2001 has been attributed to 'thugs' hired at considerable expense by wealthy and powerful men to ensure economic and political success (Lawson, 2008). President Bongo and his government have refused, until recently, to publicly acknowledge or denounce the murders. Reporters Without Borders has found that local journalists who investigate the ritual killings have been interrogated and punished by local authorities, and the subject is generally considered taboo in the national media (Reporters Without Borders, 2012).

The trigger for Anonymous's involvement in Gabon occurred in early April 2013, when Gabonese protestors were denied government permission to publicly march against the practice of ritual killing. The discovery in March of a young girl's mutilated body on a beach had reignited public anger about ritual killings, but non-government organisations representing the families of the victims had been unsuccessful in their attempts to prompt the authorities to investigate the crimes. Freedom of speech is one of the core mobilising principles of Anonymous and has been at issue in many of their activist interventions. When protestors were denied permission to march, Anonymous offered to use social media to publicise the ritual crimes. 'Operation Gabon' was announced on 7 April 2013 by a Pastebin press release explaining the practice of ritual killing and implicating Gabonese politicians. The Pastebin document included the contact details of the Gabonese president and parliament, as well as the United Nations Human Rights Council, and readers were encouraged to 'Call, fax, email (FLOOD, SPAM, ANNOY) demanding that URGENT action be IMMEDIATELY taken to stop ritual killings in Gabon and bring perpetrators to justice'.[1] The circulation of the document coincided with the uploading of a YouTube video in which Anonymous linked the ritual killings to the machinations of the country's corrupt political elite, and emphasised the relative silence of the world media and the strengthening of US–Gabon diplomatic ties despite apparent increases in ritual killings. The video threatened that, if the people of Gabon were prevented from protesting against the ritual killings, Anonymous would be protesting for them.

Using the hashtag #OpGabon, Twitter, Facebook and Tumblr users began to circulate English and French language blogs written by African activists about the ritual killings as well as graphic photos of the mutilated bodies of victims. Social media users were encouraged to participate in a 'tweetstorm' on 13 April 2013, the scheduled day on which Gabonese activists had planned their protests.[2] The 'tweetstorm' offered an alternative means of publicity for concerns about ritual killing that were otherwise being suppressed by the Gabonese government. Spurred on by Anonymous's support, some Gabonese activists undertook an unauthorised march on 13 April through the streets of Libreville, taking photos of the march and uploading them to Twitter where they were widely circulated by Anonymous. This march coincided with protests on the same day by the Gabonese diaspora in France that was also documented on social media (France24, 2013).

The interlinked protests and OpGabon social media activity catalysed significant shifts in the government's stance on ritual killing. In an apparent concession, President Bongo released a statement that obliquely acknowledged public concern about the ritual crimes (Lepoint, 2014). This was followed by more specific statements from Bongo's wife Sylvia Bongo denouncing the ritual killings. She announced that she would be leading another rally against ritual killing that had been organised by human rights activists on 22 May 2013, and that the rally would close with President Bongo making his first public speech on the issue. Local activists accused her of co-opting their march, and they arranged a separate and non-authorised march on the same day. Both marches went ahead although the non-authorised march was broken up with tear gas, and a number of key human rights leaders were arrested. These activities were detailed by OpGabon and photos were circulated on Twitter.

In June 2013, in an attempt to reduce local and international pressure on the regime, Gabonese authorities arrested former Senator Eyeghe Ekomic for failing to appear before a judge after receiving a court order regarding his alleged involvement in ritual murder. Eyomic had previously been accused by a convicted killer of ordering the 2009 ritual murder of a 12-year-old girl for 20 million francs, or approximately US\$35 000. Initially, Ekomic was protected from prosecution by parliamentary immunity but was not indicted even when the immunity was lifted after public outcry in December 2012. Following the unauthorised street protest, Ekomic was detained for nine months before being released without charge, dying suddenly at home in July 2014 a few months after his release.

The ritual killings in Gabon had received relatively limited coverage in the Western media or attention from human rights agencies prior to these coordinated online and street protests. As OpGabon unfolded, the ritual killings and protests against them were covered by a range of agencies including Reuters, Associated Press and the BBC. The ritual killings began to be prioritised by human rights agencies. For example, Freedom House is a US-based non-government organisation whose influential annual report *Freedom in the World* assesses and ranks each country according to their degree of political freedom and civil liberty. Freedom House reports mentioned ritual killings only briefly and in the last paragraph of reports from 2009–2012, and not at all in 2013 (Freedom House 2014). The 2014 report highlighted the 2013 public protests and identifies ritual killings as amongst the most serious human rights issues in Gabon, and continued to give precedence to the issue in its most recent 2015 report (Freedom House 2015). In August 2015, the US-based Human Rights Foundation criticised Argentine football star Lionel Messi for visiting Gabon at Bongo's invitation. Messi is a UNICEF Ambassador for children's rights, and the Human Rights Foundation triggered significant global media attention when they accused him of helping to 'whitewash a tyrant who has refused to investigate the disturbing ritual murders of children' (Human Rights Foundation, 2015). This unprecedented degree of attention to the issue of ritual killings in Gabon has been attributed in African media to the 2013 protests with the intervention and support of Anonymous (Lebur, 2013).

OpDeathEaters

By the close of 2014, OpGabon began to evolve into a more expansive international 'operation' that Anonymous dubbed OpDeathEaters.

OpDeathEaters takes its name from the Death Eaters, the villains of the popular Harry Potter series of books and movies known for their practice of the dark arts. The name also harks back to the terminology of OpGabon, where the perpetrators of ritual crimes were sometimes called 'heart eaters' and 'baby eaters'. Under OpDeathEaters, the links drawn in OpGabon between social inequality, political corruption and sadistic sexual abuse began to be generalised more broadly to global capitalism. Anonymous argued that the impunity that enabled the Gabonese ruling class to prey on the children of the poor is not a feature of a particular country or limited to the Global South, but rather is present in most if not all countries characterised by structural inequality, including those in the Global North.

OpDeathEaters emerged alongside mainstream press reporting of a series of rolling scandals in the UK in the wake of Jimmy Savile's death in 2011. Savile was a major figure in pop culture in the UK for almost 50 years. Following his death, at least 450 different people have contacted the authorities alleging sexual abuse by Savile (Gray and Watt, 2014). A report into the allegations made against Savile in his lifetime identified at least seven potentially actionable complaints that police failed to act on dating back to 1963 (HMIC, 2013). Savile was also named prior to his death in a major investigation into organised sexual abuse, where multiple children identified Savile amongst a number of other prominent figures alleged to have attended sexual abuse parties at 'posh' houses (Cowburn, 2012). It has become apparent that Savile was a prolific sex offender whose abuse of children and adults was overlooked by a range of institutions and authorities.

One of the earliest mentions of OpDeathEaters on social media was in reference to a disturbing anecdote contained in the British National Health Service report into Jimmy Savile's activities in public hospitals, released in November 2014 (Proctor et al., 2014). Savile had access to the mortuary at Leeds General Infirmary and expressed a fascination for dead bodies, with one former nurse reporting that Savile claimed to have sexually interfered with the corpses there (Proctor et al., 2014: 97). Two former hospital employees recounted that Savile wore rings with large, bulbous glass eyes set in them, and that Savile stated he had removed the eyes from dead bodies at the Leeds mortuary (Proctor et al., 2014: 96). A medallion set with a large glass eye was sold at a charity auction just prior to his death, and there are multiple photos of Savile taken throughout his career with large rings set with glass eyes (Robinson, 2014). For activists associated with Anonymous, Savile's necrotic jewellery closely resembled the Gabonese talismans crafted from dead bodies highlighted in OpGabon. Reports of Savile's activities with the dead prompted one of the earliest uses of the hashtag #OpDeathEaters on social media (Figure 6.1).

This tweet expressed the emerging critique that Anonymous was developing around sadistic sexual abuse as a problem shared by the Global North as much as the Global South. OpDeathEaters signalled that Anonymous was expanding their focus from Gabon to address

Heather Marsh
@GeorgieBC

Tell me the difference between this & other ritual killings.Or what it has to do with sex.
dailymail.co.uk/news/article-2…
#OpDeatheaters #CSAinquiry

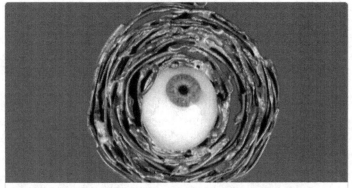

Glass eye stolen from corpse by Savile sold at charity auction for £75
It is believed to have been worn by the paedophile DJ as he co-presented the final episode of Top of the Pops at BBC Television Centre in 2006, where he also gro...
dailymail.co.uk

FIGURE 6.1

organised abuse in the United Kingdom, the United States and other supposedly 'developed' countries. In this tweet, activist Heather Marsh takes particular umbrage at the linked article's reference to Savile as a 'paedophile'. She rejects the media framing of Savile's sadistic (and apparently necrophilic) offending, and his lifelong impunity from punishment, in terms of sexual offending. Central to the OpDeathEaters campaign was an analysis of elite sexual deviance as a symptom of global inequality and exploitation rather than sexual psychopathology.

OpDeathEaters gathered steam as police investigations into Savile's abuses triggered allegations against other male celebrities, leading to the prosecution and conviction of prominent figures including Gary Glitter, Max Clifford and Rolf Harris. In a series of explosive developments throughout 2013 and 2014, Labour party politicians including now-Deputy Leader Tom Watson alleged the existence of a paedophile network in the 1980s with close connections to Westminster. Currently, a major public inquiry is underway alongside police investigations into sexual abuse allegations against politicians and other so-called VIPs ('very important people'). These reports have been shocking to British nationalism and self-identity, triggering considerable backlash in the mass media against those making the allegations and the police for investigating them. There are a number of similar scandals evident in the United States and elsewhere, where a pattern of media coverage and backlash has also been evident (Cheit, 2014; Salter, 2013b; Middleton, 2015).

There is a general lack of consensus in the public sphere about what allegations of elite deviance and organised abuse mean, and whether they should be taken seriously or dismissed as conspiracy theories. Social media provides an alternative forum for assessment and analysis. As a key figure in OpDeathEaters, Heather Marsh drew on Anonymous's experiences in OpGabon to situate the sexual abuse scandals of the UK within macro-social patterns of inequality. On her blog,[3] Marsh argued that global power structures have produced a political and economic elite with amoral or sociopathic tendencies who are effectively above the law. According to her, profoundly unequal global systems of power facilitate and encourage elite sexual violence, including the sadistic abuse of children, as a form of terrorisation that has a key role in the maintenance and reproduction of those systems.

OpDeathEaters roundly rejected descriptions of 'sexual abuse' or 'paedophilia' on the basis that these terms conflated oppressive violence with sexual desire, preferring the term 'paedosadism' to describe adults who take pleasure in harming children. Evident throughout the language and arguments of OpDeathEaters is a synthesis of Marxist thought on capitalist alienation with a feminist critique of sexual violence as an expression of power. Sadistic sexual violence emerges in this analysis as a core feature of contemporary power relations, and therefore the exposure of elite organised abuse is a potential fulcrum for global transformation. A common slogan circulated by OpDeathEaters is shown in Figure 6.2.

 **OpDeathEaters**
@OpDeathEaters

 Following

'Lift the pedosadist / trafficking networks and the entire global oligarchy will be in the net.' #OpDeathEaters

RETWEETS	LIKES	
78	27	

1:45 AM - 22 Nov 2014

FIGURE 6.2

This critique of sadistic violence as the symptom of global inequality was supplemented in OpDeathEaters by an anarchist insistence on flat, leaderless movements in which *'every person is allowed to speak and the crowd chooses both who to amplify and what actions to shun'*[4] which has been a feature of recent social movements (emphasis in original). The political framework of OpDeathEaters and its language of 'paedosadism' found purchase amongst the online networks associated with Anonymous. Dozens of OpDeathEaters accounts sprung up on Twitter, Facebook and Tumblr as Marsh encouraged social media users to collate and disseminate information on 'paedosadism' in their region or country. By January 2015, OpDeathEaters was attracting mainstream press attention, particularly in the UK where it was covered by *The Telegraph*, the *Independent* and the *Mirror*. As a social media initiative, OpDeathEaters has been successful in terms of the sheer amount of social media activity and its geographical coverage, with affiliated Twitter and Facebook accounts documenting sexual offences against children in numerous countries.

However, it has been difficult for OpDeathEaters to mobilise street protests or the formation of more enduring activist structures. 13 February 2015 was nominated as a 'day of action' for OpDeathEaters and 15 sites were identified for street protests, mostly in the United States and UK. Facebook event pages were set up to arrange and publicise each protest. It was typical for hundreds of people to nominate that they would attend; however, attendance at each event appears to have been limited to a dozen or less activists. This pattern recurred a few months later when an OpDeathEaters protest was organised in the UK to coincide with the London Marathon on 26 April 2015, which was attended by a small group of activists. Locally based OpDeathEaters groups were encouraged to set up an 'independent, victim-led inquiry/tribunal' that could collate and assess the available evidence and take testimony from victims and survivors, with the goal of putting pressure on national authorities to investigate and prosecute sexual abuse by the powerful. This is a time and resource intensive activity (and a legally fraught one at that) that received much in-principle support on social media but has yet to eventuate. Over the last 12 months, many OpDeathEaters social media accounts on Twitter and other platforms have become inactive amidst a general sense of uncertainty about the direction of the operation. The hashtag remains relatively active on Twitter and continues to highlight allegations of sexual abuse against the powerful and well-connected, although frustration at the pace of the operation has begun to show. A key goal of OpDeathEaters was the integration of information about child abuse into an open source and interactive database that could assist civilian investigations into the organised and sadistic abuse of children. The lack of volunteers to work on a project of this scale has led to multiple delays, and on 14 January 2015, the main American Twitter account of OpDeathEaters, @OpDeathEatersUS, signed off with the tweet shown as Figure 6.3.

 **OpDeathEatersUS**
@OpDeathEatersUS

#OpDeathEaters Progress is stalled w/o a database, and I'm offline until we have one. Hopefully not another year! Take care.

RETWEETS	LIKES
12	3

2:42 AM - 14 Jan 2016

FIGURE 6.3

Comparison and analysis

This chapter does not support simplistic stereotypes of lazy social media 'hacktivism' or 'clicktivism' as politically irrelevant or a substitute for 'real' political action. Instead, OpGabon and OpDeathEaters demonstrate that new frames of and responses to crime can emerge from within the transnational circulation of communication sponsored by social media. In this process, many of the limitations associated with the mass mediated public sphere – notably the asymmetrical relationship between content producers and audiences, the marginalisation of subordinate and subaltern groups, and hegemonic representation of issues of gender, race and class – are ameliorated by a more inclusive distribution of communicative power. In both operations, an international multitude of interlocutors from activists to hackers to journalists to victims and survivors participated in the development and circulation of suppressed information, as well as analyses that situated abuse and violence within an evolving political critique. As the horizons of public opinion are expanded beyond the bounds of the nation state, circumventing the formal regulation and informal conventions of the mass media, new understandings of crime and justice can develop that defy entrenched assumptions about the transparency and security of the nation state that public opinion is now exceeding.

A key aspect of both initiatives was a view of the democratic state as striated by invisible but influential allegiances that have co-opted legitimate mechanisms of power. Linkages between sadistic abuse, corruption and structural inequality can be advanced relatively easily in relation to Gabon, and global awareness of the failures of the Bongo regime have been sharpened by OpGabon and the associated protests. The transposition of this analysis to the Global North by OpDeathEaters, however, was a radical development for a number of reasons. It is undoubtedly true that Western powers such as the United Kingdom, the United States and Australia enjoy greater stability and democratic accountability than Gabon, which for some commentators lends confidence to their assertions that elite organised sexual abuse could not, and would not, emerge in so-called First World contexts. However, the developments highlighted by OpDeathEaters, particularly in the UK, undermine this confidence. Investigations are ongoing but the sheer volume of the evidence available to date challenges taken-for-granted assumptions about the internal coherence of the nation state, and suggests that the outright dismissal of allegations of elite sexual abuse can no longer be justified (Middleton, 2015).

Discernable in the shift from OpGabon to OpDeathEaters was a process of counter-colonisation as a critique of the politics of sadistic violence was transposed from the Global South to the Global North. It is more common for conceptualisations of crime and justice to be developed in the metropoles of the Global North and then used as frames for articulating both the problems facing the Global South and the solutions to them (Connell, 2007). In OpDeathEaters, the analysis of elite sexual deviance that emerged in ObGabon in partnership with local Gabonese human rights activists was exported and generalised to encompass the Global North. This defies taken-for-granted distinctions between 'developed' and 'under-developed' countries and challenges the ways in which this distinction maps onto colonialist understandings of the 'civilised' and the 'barbarous'. In the mass media and academic literature of the Global North, sadistic sexual violence is often relegated to the supposedly uncivilised countries in the Global South and, increasingly, their diaspora and other ethnic and religious minority groups (Salter, 2008). OpDeathEaters dramatically reversed this polarity and situated the organised and sadistic abuse of children at the heart of the power structures of contemporary and supposedly civilised nation states. In this process, OpGabon was retrospectively envisioned as just the first OpDeathEaters initiative (Figure 6.4):

Heather Marsh
@GeorgieBC

☼

The people of the UK have so much more in common with the people of Gabon than they ever dreamed. @opGabon #CSAinquiry #OpDeathEaters

RETWEETS   LIKES
6   3

9:06 AM - 24 Nov 2014

↩   ⟳   ♥   •••

FIGURE 6.4

What was a widely accepted link between structural inequality, legal impunity and violence against children in Gabon emerges as a potentially prescient analysis of organised sexual abuse around the globe. In this case, it seems that social media provided a 'potentially recompositional space' in which the 'atomization' of information by the boundaries of the nation state and the hegemonic frames of the mass media can be 'counteracted', generating autonomous insights that would be unlikely to form within the mass media (Dyer-Witheford, 1999: 127).

Of the two initiatives, OpGabon most clearly illustrates the potential of social media to make significant contributions to emancipatory social and political movements. One of the challenges identified by Fraser (2014) in her analysis of transnational public opinion is that it is not always clear who or what it is addressed to, and who is obliged to act on it. In this case of ObGabon, the initiative had multiple addressees: the Gabonese human rights activists that Anonymous assured had their support, the families and communities of the victims of ritual killings, the Gabonese regime which Anonymous repeatedly threatened with exposure and other reprisals, other interested social media users, and what might be broadly called the international press and civil society. While only the Gabonese regime constitutes here a 'strong public' with the capability (although not the will) to implement public opinion, OpGabon was able to enhance and mobilise the 'soft power' of civil society and press. The enduring legacy of OpGabon is the increased prominence of the issue of ritual killings and the ongoing pressure on Gabon and its allies to respond. Without the intervention of Anonymous, it's possible that the wave of protests in 2013 might never have occurred. In personal communication with the author, Heather Marsh (2015, personal communication) emphasised that, while OpGabon was always a partnership between Gabonese human rights activists and Anonymous, Anonymous's intervention was decisive in empowering local activists.

> The initial march we were supporting was small and in fact had decided it would be futile to continue with the march until they saw the backing from Anonymous. Being an activist against ritual killings in a country which jails you for suggesting they exist has never attracted a lot of people.

Empowering and emboldening local activism was crucial to the success of OpGabon. OpGabon was facilitated by a groundswell of long-standing discontent with the regime in Gabon and the existence of multiple organisations within African civil society concerned about ritual killings. In contrast, OpDeathEaters found it difficult to mobilise beyond a network of online activists. Core to the emotional resonance of the movement was the orchestration of an 'us vs them' solidarity common to contemporary social movements such as Occupy, albeit with a focus on perverse sexuality. Anonymous framed the 'Death Eaters' as the elite but sexually deviant 1 per cent that the rest of us – the 99 per cent – have an obligation to resist. However, 'Death Eaters' and 'paedosadism' were concepts unique to Anonymous who rejected the more common terminology of 'sexual abuse' and 'paedophilia' used by many non-government organisations and advocates in the area of child abuse. This may have made it harder for OpDeathEaters to form links within civil society or engage anti-abuse activists. There were other challenges facing OpDeathEaters' attempts at broader mobilisation, including the degree of traumatisation evident amongst survivors of organised abuse, and the absence of a 'higher power' that specifically advocates on their behalf. Reflecting on the two operations, Marsh (2015, personal communication) observed that OpDeathEaters encountered different challenges than OpGabon:

Gabon also has a political opposition which can leverage ritual killings as evidence of the corruption of the existing power and present an alternative. Part of the added challenge I see for OpDeathEaters in countries like the UK and US...is there is no higher power for people to turn to, they have to create one. That of course requires far more widespread mobilization and initiative than what OpGabon is doing, [such as] political lobbying, supporting the opposition, and appealing for outside intervention in the form of the ICC [International Criminal Court] or boycotts. It [OpDeathEaters] also requires mobilization of the weakest members of society, the survivors, since no political party or institution exists which can be trusted to fight on their behalf. Also, while mainstream media (which is just as influential in Africa as elsewhere) is very willing to accept that 'ritual killings' exist in Africa, they are far more opposed to campaigns exposing corruption in their own circles.

A comparison of the two operations suggests that social media can sponsor new discursive formations about crime and justice that can flow in unexpected ways through the transnational circuits of public opinion enabled by social media. The effects of these discourses and points of consensus, however, differ according to the contexts in which they are developed and received. OpGabon amplified and sustained the efforts of an established network of human rights activists in Gabon, and, as Marsh observes above, the mass media was sympathetic to these efforts since it is already attuned to narratives of ritual and sadistic violence in Africa. In contrast, OpDeathEaters had the more ambitious task of catalysing a global social movement and generating publicity for disavowed forms of child sexual abuse that the mass media has previously ignored or rejected as false allegations. At this point, OpDeathEaters has gathered and distributed a significant amount of information on organised sexual abuse, but it remains to be seen whether it will find critical purchase on the social realities of organised sexual abuse in local contexts. Nonetheless, Marsh (2015, personal communication) attributes a number of successes to OpDeathEaters, particularly an increased receptivity in the public and mass media to stories of elite sexual deviance, and the countering of 'propaganda' that minimises the seriousness of child sexual abuse and denies the existence of organised abusive networks.

Conclusion

In her reformulation of public sphere theory in a global world, Fraser (2014) suggests that the fact that transnational public opinion does not always correlate to 'strong publics' that can act on those opinions does not discredit those public discourses that are emerging via new media technologies. She emphasises the normative legitimacy of publics that are capable of expanding to enable equal participation by all those affected by increasingly complex global systems and structures. Certainly, OpGabon and OpDeathEaters appear to meet this criteria through their expansiveness and inclusiveness, and their analysis of the complex historical and transnational systems and institutions that contribute to structural inequality within and beyond the nation state. The question of their political efficacy is more complex. However, for Fraser (2014), to observe the emergence of transnational public spheres in the absence of transnational public powers is not to discredit those public spheres, but instead it highlights the need for mechanisms of power that are responsive to new formations of public opinion as a vitally important, albeit absent, constitutive element for a truly democratic international order.

As social media operations, OpGabon and OpDeathEaters were effective in raising the public profile and awareness of organised forms of elite deviance and sadistic violence even though they differed in their purchase within established political and social movements. Marsh's argument that OpDeathEaters was ahead of its time in the sense that it was not simply addressing a 'higher power' (that is, established institutions such as non-government organisations or investigatory bodies) but rather calling for survivors of abuse and their allies to generate their own is compelling. The operation functioned by drawing disparate social media users into a loose coalition and encouraging them to drive localised action in relation to sadistic abuse. This constitutes what Gerbaudo (2012) has called the 'choreography of assembly' of social media protest, 'a process of symbolic and material gathering or assembling, staged against the situation of spatial dispersion which characterises post-industrial societies' (p. 15). In this process, social media provides 'not simply channels of information but also crucial *emotional conduits* through which organisers have condensed individual sentiments of indignation, anger, pride and a sense of shared victimhood' (p. 14, original emphasis).

However, time will tell whether the socio-political framing of sadistic abuse offered by Anonymous will find a wider audience. Research and advocacy into elite organised abuse is ongoing, and Middleton (2015) suggests that evidence of organised and sadistic abuse has accumulated to the point where a 'tipping point' has been reached and denial is no longer a viable defence mechanism. Contributing to this tipping point is the international circulation of information and evidence that points to a problem beyond the boundaries of any particular location or nation state. While media focus has been trained on particular cases or regions in an isolated fashion, public understanding of organised abuse has lacked a broader framework of understanding. Social media expands the circulation of information and discourse in ways that facilitate such an understanding, and this has been reworked by activists such as Marsh in order to propose radical re-interpretations of child abuse and torture as a symptom of political pathology. At the same time, the geographical dispersal of social media users can also inhibit the translation of shared discourse into political action, which appeared to be the case in OpDeathEaters. This suggests that social media cannot replace struggles 'on the ground' and its ties may be too weak to act as the sole catalyst of political mobilisation. Rather, it is most effective as 'a medium within which terrestrial struggles can be made visible and linked with one another' (Dyer-Witheford, 1999: 128).

Notes

1 http://pastebin.com/b69rhF13.
2 A 'tweetstorm' involves a coordinated spike in social media activity on Twitter using an agreed upon hashtag, which is designed to amplify social media and mass media coverage.
3 https://georgiebc.wordpress.com.
4 https://georgiebc.wordpress.com/2014/11/08/the-other-battle-for-the-inter net/?utm_content=buffer25d05&utm_medium=social&utm_source=twitter. com&utm_campaign=buffer.

Suggested links

OpGabon on Twitter: https://twitter.com/opgabon.
OpDeathEaters on Twitter: https://twitter.com/OpDeathEaters.
Heather Marsh's (Twitter: @GeorgieBC) blog: https://georgiebc.wordpress.com.

CONCLUSION

Michael Salter
@mike_salter

Ugh writing a critical history of #gamergate for the new book - mob #MRA stupidity on a grand scale.

RETWEETS   LIKES
17   19

7:03 PM - 3 Jun 2015

FIGURE 7.1

While writing Chapter 2, I sent this tweet (Figure 7.1) using the #Gamergate hashtag. By this point, I had spent two months trying to untangle the complex chronology of Gamergate and the ever-expanding justifications offered by angry gamers for a consistent pattern of misogynist abuse and harassment. My tweeted reference to #MRA ('men's rights activists') felt justified. I'd been studying men's rights activists and other anti-feminist 'backlash' groups for a long time, and there were many parallels with the Gamergate movement: men claiming they were 'under attack' by women and minority groups, allegations of a feminist and 'politically correct' conspiracy, vituperative attacks on the careers and reputations of women and their supporters rationalised as necessary 'truth-telling' and cleansing of the body politic. I sent the tweet to see what my 'followers' and others thought of Gamergate. I thought I might get a few angry responses from 'gators; a couple of dozen, at most.

Within two hours, I must have received a few hundred insults and threats. My phone 'blew up' over the next four days. I was called a 'white knight', a 'cuck' and a 'mangina', common right-wing insults reserved for men considered gender and race traitors for holding progressive views. One 'gator opened a Pastebin account and encouraged others to scour the internet and my social media accounts to collate potentially compromising data to embarrass or blackmail me. Although this attempt to create a 'dirt file' proved fruitless, it was disconcerting to think that a cluster of random strangers might be trawling through my internet history. Meanwhile abuse and insults were accumulating too quickly for me to read or respond. I couldn't reply to even a fraction of the users contacting me, which they often took as a personal insult and justification for further abuse, and there were too many to block. I couldn't use Twitter in any normal way while this storm was ongoing. Each morning I would wake up to reams of abusive tweets and they would continue through the day.

My taste of 'gator fury was the tiniest fraction of what has been directed at women such as Zoe Quinn and Anita Sarkeesian. After two or three days, the 'gators found new target/s. To prevent a recurrence, I installed Randi Lee Harper's 'good game auto blocker', which, as Chapter 2 mentions, is a piece of free software that enables Twitter users to block the thousands of accounts active within the Gamergate movement. Life went on. I wasn't sent rape threats, 'dick pics' or sexually aggressive messages, which are typical of the abusive content received by female social media users. I didn't have to endure images of lynchings or the anti-Semitic or Islamaphobic material often used to harass social media users from other racial or cultural backgrounds. While the content I was sent was offensive, I was subject to relatively little intrusive behaviour such as doxing or stalking. This was an unusual flare-up in my social media activity, which is mostly collegial even in disagreement.

I suspect that the main reason this incident passed so quickly is because I'm a white man, and you can tell this from my profile picture. My personal characteristics don't lend themselves to the attempts at stigmatisation and humiliation that are used to drive women and diverse users from online publics. The backdrop of online prejudice is what activates the transformation of a localised flurry of abuse into a full-blown viral campaign, at which point the quantified metrics of social media provide an abusive 'score card' by which participants in the campaign can measure their 'wins'. This process is harder to set in train for social media users like me, to the point where even dedicated online harassers don't put a lot of effort in. This has the effect of, first, increasing the burden of abuse and harassment on already oppressed groups, and second, creating a significant disincentive to public participation and entrenching unequal representation in the public sphere. Recently, television producer Amanda Collinge (2016) explained that a reason for the lack of female guests on the politically influential Australian television programme Q&A is that many women decline the invitation due to 'the well-founded fear that the online abuse and harassment they already suffer will increase'. Online abuse is not just personally impactful; it is politically consequential, and requires a response that is commensurate to the threat that it poses to individual safety and equality of participation in public life.

This book has argued that online abuse emerges from within the recursive relationship between technological design, social patterns and struggles, and the worldviews and practices of social agents. Responding to online abuse requires a staggered and flexible approach that addresses its subpolitical and subcriminal manifestations, as well as its more obviously criminal forms. What follows are five suggested areas for addressing the prevalence of online abuse that seek to integrate protection, prevention, support and deterrence as key principles for the response to online abuse.

Law enforcement and reform

While policing agencies have invested heavily in certain areas of online law enforcement, they often lack the capacity or motivation to investigate adult complaints of online abuse. Even where online abuse takes clearly illegal forms, such as in the case of rape or death threats, users report widespread disinterest and lack of understanding from law enforcement. Many forms of online abuse are already covered by existing laws but these are frequently not enforced. There is a need for improved training of law enforcement officers on the forms and impact of online abuse, and for investment of law enforcement resources into the investigation and prosecution of online abuse. Where existing laws are insufficient, then law reform is an important mechanism through which to sanction offenders, deter others and clearly communicate community disapproval of online abuse. However an over-reliance on criminalisation can have counterproductive effects, as has been evident where minors have been charged under child pornography statutes for making images of their own bodies (Salter et al., 2013). Furthermore, much of the impact of online abuse comes from its pervasive but subpolitical force; that is, the persistence of subcriminal abuse from large numbers of users acting on a shared hostility to one user or a particular group of users. As Shanley Kane, founder and CEO of Model View Culture, an independent media platform that addresses diversity in online culture and technology, put it: 'There's the constant background, opportunistic, low-grade harassment – responses to my tweets that are deliberately using hate speech, sexist slurs and words, or juvenile trolling' (quoted in Gandy, 2014). The fact that such abuse may not meet a criminal threshold does not mean it does not exert individual or collective effects. Law enforcement and reform is thus an important part of the response to online abuse but will not solve it.

Social media design

When instantiated with instrumental logics, the 'technological rationality' (Marcuse, 1964) of social media can generate an objectifying milieu of which abuse and harassment is a likely outcome. However, this rationality is not inherent in social media but rather reflects the values and principles that underpin software interfaces and architecture to make abuse more likely. It is possible, therefore, to design platforms that proactively dissuade users from such practices and encourage an ethos of mutual care. For example, Yik Yak is a social media app launched in 2013, which allows for anonymous short postings ('yaks') that are restricted to a local area. It's similar to Twitter except that there is no user profile, no list of 'followers', and yaks are only visible to those within a 2.5 kilometre radius. On Yik Yak, there is no self-brand to construct and promote, and no quantified measures of individual popularity to publicly rank users against one another. As a result, Yik Yak does not support the kinds of status-building and jostling evident on other platforms that often gives rise to abuse, and it's local focus prevents abusive content from going viral in any meaningful sense. While users may attempt to use Yik Yak to bully another user, the scope of the abuse is delimited by the local focus of the application.

Yik Yak's design also empowers other users to bring abuse to an end. The interface includes an 'up vote' or a 'down vote' for each yak. Funny or appealing yaks receive 'up votes', which increases the prominence of the 'yak' in the local area. However, comments that receive more than five 'down' votes are automatically deleted. This enables a swift bystander response to abusive content, unlike other platforms where bystanders can typically do very little to stop online abuse unfolding. Yik Yak also calculates a 'Yakarma' score for each individual user (visible only to that user) that rewards those who receive a high number of 'up votes'. While Yakarma arguably creates incentives for users to generate shocking or provocative content to attract 'up votes', it sanctions persistent abusers whose yaks are regularly attracting 'down votes'. Yik Yak has instituted other robust anti-abuse measures. After widespread misuse of the app in schools for cyber-bullying, Yik Yak now places 'geofencing' around high schools in the United States, which prevents students from accessing the app on campus. Content moderators remove content 'flagged' as abusive by users, and are supported by automatic filters and algorithms that attempt to prevent the posting of full names and other potentially inappropriate content.

While there have been a number of media reports of bullying and harassment on Yik Yak, particularly on college campuses, the possibility of down-voting abusive comments into oblivion can encourage the formation of a protective culture amongst local users (Junco, 2015). Far from excluding or marginalising subaltern users, Hess (2015a) argues that Yik Yak can amplify the voices of women and sexually and racially diverse groups, and enable users to discuss taboo topics in a constructive fashion. She describes a number of protective interventions emerging spontaneously on college campuses via Yik Yak, including an instance in which expressions of support for suicidal users on the platform coalesced into a campus rally for increased mental health resources, and another case where reports that two men had been ejected from a nightclub for kissing generated a 'kiss in' protest inside the club. This illustrates the availability of social media for a multiplicity of uses, and the ways in which particular design features can be disenabling of abuse while promoting more constructive forms of sociability.

Education

In focus groups, young people reported that 'cyber-safety' messages from their schools and families were often counterproductive. A simple focus on online 'risk reduction' can responsibilise girls and women for managing the risk of online abuse, which reinforces victim-blaming attitudes and exculpating perpetrators of online abuse of responsibility (Salter et al., 2013). This often dovetails with an 'abstinence' approach to online sexual expression, in which any sexualised self-representation or interaction through social media is construed as inordinately threatening to (typically female) safety and reputation (Dobson and Ringrose, 2016). Such approaches ignore the normalisation of online sexual expression through popular social media dating and 'hook up' applications such as Tindr and Grindr. For a significant number of teenagers and adults, making and sharing 'nude' or suggestive images of themselves has become a regular feature of their intimate lives and practices, albeit one that is underpinned by familiar double standards in moral assessments of male and female behaviour. Instructing young people to abstain from making or sharing intimate images fails to provide them with the skills to negotiate the significant shifts that social media has catalysed in sexual cultures, or the evident continuity in sexist norms and values that persist in intimate image-making and exchange.

Rather than viewing it as a threat or risk to young people, the self-production of social media content can be understood as an important pedagogical opportunity to open up critical discussions about media production and consumption with young people, including the impacts of consumer culture, pornography and social media (Dobson,

2015). Integrating discussions of social media into curricula focused on sexual ethics and the negotiation of consent (see Carmody, 2013) is a step in the right direction and recognises the embeddedness of social media in peer and intimate relations. For example, the Australian primary prevention campaign 'The Line' aims to reduce intimate abuse and coercion and promote respectful relationships (www.theline.org.au). Rather than instructing young people to 'just say no' to sexting, the website offers advice on how to frame an image to minimise the potential for harm, such as 'Keep your face OUT of the image and make sure it's not recognisable as you'. Other advice includes sending a sexy text message or provocative emoji as a substitute for a 'nude'. The site also recommends that young people download 'Send this instead', an app that provides users with images that they can send as humorous responses to unwanted requests for a 'nude'. This advice is embedded within a larger focus on increasing young people's capacity to develop mutually beneficial peer and intimate relationships. Furnishing young people with multiple strategies to prevent online abuse and negotiate technologically mediated relationships is likely to be far more effective in reducing online abuse than punitive or shaming responses to young people's online practices.

Support options

The development of support options for victims of online abuse is integral to an adequate response. At present, support is being offered by existing victim services and by largely volunteer or crowdfunded online organisations. Rape crisis and domestic violence services have been reporting the increasing use of social media and networked technologies by perpetrators to stalk, threaten and harass victims, which has required them to upskill and expand their service offerings (Southworth et al., 2007). Online abuse victims have mobilised online to provide support and advocacy for others. As Chapter 2 discussed, Zoe Quinn's 'Crash Override Network' and Randi Lee Harper's 'Online Abuse Prevention Initiative' arose out of their respective experiences of Gamergate harassment. In the United States, women victimised through the non-consensual circulation of intimate images have formed a number of advocacy groups which have played a major role in criminalising some forms of 'revenge porn' and driving increased responsivity from the authorities (Salter and Crofts, 2015). Hollaback! is an organisation that opposes harassment in public places, and has developed the HeartMob (https://iheartmob.org), where people can report an incident of online abuse, receive support and advice, and request that 'heartmobbers' (volunteers who are screened and registered by the website) intervene in the abuse on the site.

There is an argument to be made that, since online abuse is a frequent byproduct of social media, then social media platforms should be providing funding to victim support groups to ensure they remain viable and active, and can offer a continuity of care to victims. After all, social media users are the 'outsourced' volunteer workforce of Web 2.0: they generate the content, interaction and 'clicks' upon which the profits of social media companies depend. Social media companies have a duty of care to users that they rarely acknowledge (except in relation to the abuse of minors). The failure of social media platforms to take responsibility for online abuse devolves the burden of harassment to users, which in turn has a flow-on effect to victim support services as well as the new organisations described above. In effect, the costs of online abuse are shifted downstream to users, support services and volunteers. As social media platforms develop a more comprehensive response to online abuse, they have a moral obligation to provide funding to the organisations and services that are addressing the harms of abuse on their platforms.

Activism and justice-seeking

In the discussion of ObGabon and OpDeathEeaters in Chapter 6, it was evident that social media offered opportunities to recognise otherwise suppressed or disavowed social problems and place those problems in a transnational frame, giving rise to new points of insight and potential intervention. Social media can generate and distribute frameworks of meaning and understanding that can empower the efforts of existing social movements and play a potential role in persuading both 'weak' and 'strong' publics to act. However, social media functions on 'communicative power' (Castells, 2009) which does not, in and of itself, have the capacity to mobilise material resources or catalyse a shift in power relations. In the absence of more durable activist or organisational structures, the emotional resonance and momentum that develops on social media can become frustrated or lost. The supposedly 'flat' or 'leaderless' structure that has characterised many contemporary social movements, and particularly those with a strong online presence, may enhance the inclusivity of the movement but is no substitute for a dedicated movement grounded in 'strong ties' between activists. It is through these activist structures that new formations of meaning on social media might exert more influence over broader public deliberation and decision-making. While social media is not the realisation of the e-democracy dreams of the cyber-utopians, its emancipatory potentialities should not be dismissed. The power of public recognition is not purely symbolic. Silence and disbelief exert corrosive effects on subaltern groups and victimised individuals whose lived experiences and needs are denied acknowledgement in the public sphere (Salter, 2012). Social media offers opportunities through which those experiences and needs can not only be aired, but subject to discussion and debate, and the formulation of potential solutions. The fact that this is accomplished within the geographically expanded discursive horizon offered by social media can, as some critics suggest, disperse or frustrate the impulse towards action, but it can also generate consequential feelings of interconnection and interdependence that would otherwise evade nationally bounded mass mediated publics.

GLOSSARY

App   Short for 'application', an 'app' usually refers to a software programme that can be downloaded by a user to a mobile device. A
'social media app' refers to the smartphone or tablet interface of a
social media platform, which may or may not also have a website.

Blogs   A blog (short for 'weblog') is a website that is regularly updated
by a user or a group of users with short written pieces or 'posts'.
Blogs are usually informal, conversational and expressive.

Channers   A slang term for users who frequent the 'chan' image boards.

Crowdfunding   Crowdfunding sites support artists and online content
creators to accumulate multiple 'patrons' who provide ongoing
funding on a recurring basis or per outwork/output. These platforms
can also enable social media users such as bloggers, vloggers and
freelance writers to generate a reliable income from their work.

Doxing/doxxing   Doxing refers to the practice of collating personally
identifying information about someone and distributing it online.

Hashtag   A hashtag refers to a word or phrase preceded by the # sign,
which can be used on social media sites to identify content on a
particular topic. Hashtags are particularly prominent on Twitter but
evident elsewhere. They enable users to search for tweets on an
issue or trending topic.

Revenge porn This is a colloquial term referring to the non-consensual online publication of intimate images of an ex-partner in the aftermath of a break-up (Salter and Crofts, 2015). The images are typically uploaded out of spite or revenge. Some commentators prefer terms such as 'digital abuse' or 'image-based sexual exploitation'.

Screenshot A screenshot is a digital image of the display of a computer screen or mobile device.

Sexting 'Sexting' refers to the taking and/or sending of self-produced sexualised images or text messages.

Trolling The term trolling has a number of meanings in internet culture. In the 1990s it referred primarily to people who 'argue for the sake of arguing' online and are disruptive on online mailing lists and platforms (Coleman, 2014: 39). The term is now used more narrowly to refer to those who consciously provoke and incite conflict online. 'Trolling' also refers to established online subcultures and networks built around abuse and causing offence (Phillips, 2015).

Vlogs A vlog is essentially a blog where postings are primary videos. YouTube is a common platform for vloggers.

REFERENCES

Aas, K. F. 2013. Beyond the 'desert of the real': crime control in a virtual(ised) reality. In: Jewkes, Y. (ed.) *Crime Online* (pp. 160–178). London & New York: Routledge.

Adest, A. 2006. Rupert Murdoch comments on Fox Interactive's growth. Seeking Alpha, August 9, http://seekingalpha.com/article/15237-rupert-murdoch-comments-on-fox-interactives-growth.

Ahn, J. 2011. Digital divides and social network sites: which students participate in social media? *Journal of Educational Computing Research.* 45(2), 147–163.

Alberty, E. 2014. Feminist media critic calls for boycott of Utah campuses. *Salt Lake Tribune,* October 16, www.sltrib.com/sltrib/news/58529300-78/sarkesian-threats-usu-austin.html.csp.

Alexander, L. 2014. 'Gamers' don't have to be your audience. 'Gamers' are over. Gamasutra, August 28, www.gamasutra.com/view/news/224400/Gamers_dont_have_to_be_your_audience_Gamers_are_over.php.

Alfonso III, F. 2014. #EndFathersDay is the work of 4chan, not feminists. Daily Dot, June 2014, www.dailydot.com/lifestyle/4chan-end-fathers-day.

Allen, J. G. 2014. How imageboard culture shaped Gamergate, Boing Boing, December 31, http://boingboing.net/2014/2012/2031/how-imageboard-culture-shaped.html.

Allen, J. 2015a. How crowdfunding helps haters profit from harassment. Boing Boing, January 14, http://boingboing.net/2015/01/14/how-crowdfunding-helps-haters.html.

Allen, J. 2015b. The invasion boards that set out to ruin lives. Boing Boing, January 19, http://boingboing.net/2015/01/19/invasion-boards-set-out-to-rui.html.

AP. 2014. Notorious 'revenge porn king' charged with hacking. *Sydney Morning Herald*, January 25, www.smh.com.au/world/notorious-revenge-porn-king-charged-with-hacking-20140125-hv9tc.html – ixzz2tFZutQrv.

AP/MTV. 2009. A thin line: 2009 AP-MTV digital abuse study. www.athinline.org/MTV-AP_Digital_Abuse_Study_Executive_Summary.pdf.

Attwood, F. 2006. Sexed up: theorizing the sexualization of culture. *Sexualities*, 9(1), 77–94.

Attwood, F. 2007. Sluts and riot grrrls: female identity and sexual agency. *Journal of Gender Studies*, 16(3), 233–247.

Auerbach, D. 2012. Anonymity as culture: treatise. *Triple Canopy*, February 9, www.canopycanopycanopy.com/contents/anonymity_as_culture__treatise.

Baio, A. 2014. 72 hours of #Gamergate: digging through 316,669 tweets from three days of Twitter's two month old trainwreck. October 27, https://medium.com/message/72-hours-of-gamergate-e00513f7cf5d.

Banet-Weiser, S. 2012. *Authentic TM: the politics and ambivalence in a brand culture*, New York: NYU Press.

Barlow, J. P. 1996. Selling wine without bottles: the economy of mind on the global net. In: Ludlow, P. (ed.), *High noon on the electronic frontier: conceptual issues in cyberspace* (pp. 9–34). Cambridge, MA: MIT Press.

Bartlett, J., Norrie, R., Patel, S., Rumpel, R. & Wibberley, S. 2014. Misogyny on Twitter. www.demos.co.uk/files/MISOGYNY_ON_TWITTER.pdf?1399567516.

Beck, U. 1997. Subpolitics ecology and the disintegration of institutional power. *Organization & Environment*, 10(1), 52–65.

Benhabib, S. 1992. Models of public space: Hannah Arendt, the liberal tradition, and Jürgen Habermas. In: Calhoun, C. (ed.), *Habermas and the public sphere* (pp. 73–99). Cambridge, MA & London: MIT Press.

Bennett, W. L., Toft, A., Chadwick, A. & Howard, P. 2009. Identity, technology, and narratives. Transnational activism and social networks. In: A. Chadwick & P. N. Howard (eds), *Routledge handbook of internet politics* (pp. 146–260). Routledge: London and New York.

Bernault, F. 2013. Carnal technologies and the double life of the body in Gabon. *Critical African Studies*, 5(3), 175–194.

Boddy, D. 2013. The Facebook generation is in the grip of National Attention Deficit Disorder. *The Telegraph*, March 4, www.telegraph.co.uk/technology/social-media/9907611/The-Facebook-generation-is-in-the-grip-of-National-Attention-Deficit-Disorder.html.

boyd, d. 2013. White flight in networked publics? How race and class shaped American teen engagement with Myspace and Facebook. In: Nakamura, L.

and Cow-White, P. A. (eds) *Race after the Internet* (pp. 203–222). New York and London: Routledge.

boyd, d. (2014). *It's complicated: the social lives of networked teens.* New Haven, CT: Yale University Press.

boyd, d. m. & Ellison, N. B. 2007. Social network sites: definition, history, and scholarship. *Journal of Computer-Mediated Communication*, 13(1), 210–230.

Brail, S. 1996. The price of admission: harassment and free speech in the wild, wild west. In: Cherny, L. & Reba Wise, E. (eds), *Wired women: gender and new realities in cyberspace* (pp. 141–157). Washington, DC: Seal Press.

Brodmerkel, S. & Carah, N. 2013. Alcohol brands on Facebook: the challenges of regulating brands on social media. *Journal of Public Affairs*, 13(3), 272–281.

Bruns, A. 2008. *Blogs, Wikipedia, Second Life, and beyond: from production to produsage*, New York & Washington: Peter Lang.

Burkett, M. & Hamilton, K. 2012. Postfeminist sexual agency: young women's negotiations of sexual consent. *Sexualities*, 15(7), 815–833.

Burns, A. 2015. Self(ie)-discipline: social regulation as enacted through the discussion of photographic practice. *International Journal of Communication*, 9, http://ijoc.org/index.php/ijoc/article/view/3138.

Caggiano, A. 2015. Man shamed for trolling Clementine Ford apologises for online attack. *Sydney Morning Herald*, June 26, www.smh.com.au/national/man-shamed-for-trolling-clementine-ford-apologises-for-online-attack-20150625-ghxz24.html.

Carmody, M. 2013. Young men, sexual ethics and sexual negotiation. *Sociological Research Online*, 18(2), 22.

Carr, N. 2008. Is Google making us stupid? What the internet is doing to our brains. *The Atlantic*, July/August, www.theatlantic.com/magazine/archive/2008/07/is-google-making-us-stupid/306868/.

Castells, M. 2009. *Communication power*, Oxford: Oxford University Press.

Castells, M. 2012. *Networks of outrage and hope*, Cambridge and Malden: Polity.

Chafkin, M. 2007. How to kill a great idea! *Inc*, June 1, www.inc.com/magazine/20070601/features-how-to-kill-a-great-idea.html.

Cheit, R. 2014. *The witch-hunt narrative: politics, psychology and the sexual abuse of children*, Oxford: Oxford University Press.

Chen, A. 2012. 4chan's moment is over even though it's more popular than ever. Gawker, December 7, http://gawker.com/5925535/4chans-moment-is-over-even-though-its-more-popular-than-ever.

Chen, A. 2013. Inside Facebook's outsourced anti-porn and gore brigade, where 'camel toes' are more offensive than 'crushed heads'. Gawker, February 16, http://gawker.com/5885714/inside-facebooks-outsourced-anti-porn-and-gore-brigade-where-camel-toes-are-more-offensive-than-crushed-heads.

Chen, A. 2014. The laborers who keep dick pics and beheadings out of your Facebook feed. *Wired*, October 23, www.wired.com/2014/10/content-moderation/.

Chmielewski, D. C. & Sarno, D. 2009. How MySpace fell off the pace. *Los Angeles Times*, June 17, http://articles.latimes.com/2009/jun/17/business/fi-ct-myspace17.

Citron, D. K. 2014. *Hate crimes in cyberspace*, Cambridge, MA and London: Harvard University Press.

Cloos, K. & Turkewitz, J. 2015. Hundreds of nude photos jolt Colorado school. *New York Times*, November 6, www.nytimes.com/2015/11/07/us/colorado-students-caught-trading-nude-photos-by-the-hundreds.html?_r=1.

Coleman, G. 2014. *Hacker, hoaxer, whistleblower, spy: the many faces of anonymous*, London: Verso Books.

Collinge, A. 2016. Producer reveals the disturbing reason why Q&A has a 'problem' with women. Mamamia, 9 February, www.mamamia.com.au/women-on-qa/.

Condis, M. 2015. No homosexuals in Star Wars? BioWare, 'gamer' identity, and the politics of privilege in a convergence culture. *Convergence: The International Journal of Research into New Media Technologies*, 21(2), 198–212.

Connell, R. 2007. *Southern theory*, Sydney: Allen & Unwin.

Consalvo, M. 2012. Confronting toxic gamer culture: a challenge for feminist game studies scholars. *Ada: A Journal of Gender, New Media, and Technology*, 1. http://adanewmedia.org/2012/11/issue1-consalvo/?utm_source=rss&utm_medium=rss&utm_campaign=issue1-consalvo.

Cook, I. 2005. Western heterosexual masculinity, anxiety, and web porn. *The Journal of Men's Studies*, 14(1), 47–63.

Cowburn, M. 2012. Reflections on the Jimmy Savile disclosures: grooming and denial behind the masks of masculinities. *British Society of Criminology Newsletter*, 71, 17–20.

Cox, C. 2014. Female games journalists quit over harassment, #GamerGate harms women. The Mary Sue, Sept 4, www.themarysue.com/gamergate-harms-women.

Cross, K. A. 2014. Ethics for Cyborgs: on real harassment in an 'unreal' place. *Loading*, 8, http://journals.sfu.ca/loading/index.php/loading/article/view/140/170.

Dahlberg, L. 2001. The internet and democratic discourse: exploring the prospects of online deliberative forums extending the public sphere. *Information, Communication & Society*, 4(4), 615–633.

Dean, J. 2010. *Blog theory: feedback and capture in the circuits of drive*, Cambridge & Malden: Polity.

Dibbell, J. 1993. A rape in cyberspace. *Village Voice*, December 23, www.juliandibbell.com/texts/bungle_vv.html.

Dibbell, J. 2009. The Assclown Offensive: how to enrage the Church of Scientology. *Wired*, September 21, http://archive.wired.com/culture/culture reviews/magazine/17-10/mf_chanology?currentPage=all.

Dobson, A. S. 2014. Laddishness online: the possible significations and significance of 'performative shamelessness' for young women in the post-feminist context. *Cultural Studies*, 28(1), 142–164.

Dobson, A. S. 2015. *Postfeminist digital cultures: femininity, social media, and self-representation*, New York: Palgrave Macmillan.

Dobson, A. S. and Ringrose, J. 2016. Sext education: pedagogies of sex, gender and shame in the schoolyards of Tagged and Exposed. *Sex Education*, 16(1), 8–21.

Dodero, C. 2012. Hunter Moore makes a living screwing you. *Village Voice*, April 4, www.villagevoice.com/news/hunter-moore-makes-a-living-screwing-you-6435187.

Dodge, A. 2016. Digitizing rape culture: online sexual violence and the power of the digital photograph. *Crime, Media, Culture*, 12(1), 65–82.

Dyer-Witheford, N. 1999. *Cyber-Marx: cycles and circuits of struggle in high-technology capitalism*, Urbana and Chicago, IL: University of Illinois Press.

Edwards, J. 2015. Twitter 'unverified' the right-winger writer Milo Yiannopoulos and nobody is behaving in a reasonable or sober manner about it. *Business Insider*, January 10, www.businessinsider.com.au/milo-yiannopoulos-nero-unverified-by-twitter-2016-1?r=UK&IR=T.

Ellison, L. 2001. Cyberstalking: tackling harassment on the internet. In: Wall, D. (ed.) *Crime and the internet* (pp. 141–152). Oxon and New York: Routledge.

Ellison, N. B., Vitak, J., Steinfield, C., Gray, R. & Lampe, C. 2011. Negotiating privacy concerns and social capital needs in a social media environment. In: Trepte, S. & Reinecke, L. (eds) *Privacy online: perspectives on privacy and self-disclosure in the social web* (pp. 19–32). New York: Springer.

Esguerra, R. 2009. Google CEO Eric Schmidt dismisses the importance of privacy. *Electronic Frontier Foundation*, December 10, www.eff.org/deeplinks/2009/12/google-ceo-eric-schmidt-dismisses-privacy.

Feenberg, A. 1996. Marcuse or Habermas: two critiques of technology 1. *Inquiry*, 39, 45–70.

Feenberg, A. 2002. *Transforming technology: a critical theory revisited*. New York: Oxford University Press.

Filipovic, J. 2015. Anita Sarkeesian is fighting to make the web less awful for women – and getting death threats in the process. *Cosmopolitan*, June 8, www.cosmopolitan.com/career/a39908/anita-sarkeesian-internets-most-fascinating.

Fine, M. 1988. Sexuality, schooling, and adolescent females: the missing discourse of desire. *Harvard Educational Review*, 58(1), 29–54.

Ford, C. 2015. Why I used a nude photo to protest Sunrise's victim blaming Facebook post. *Daily Life*, June 19, www.dailylife.com.au/news- and-views/

dl-opinion/clementine-ford-why-i-used-a-nude-photo-to-protest-sunrises-victim-blaming-facebook-post-20150619-ghsd4k.html.

France24. 2013. Anonymous stands for Gabonese victims of ritual crimes. France24, April 15, http://article.wn.com/view/2013/04/15/Anonymous_stands_for_Gabonese_victims_of_ritual_crimes/.

Frank, J. 2014. How to attack a woman who works in video gaming. *The Guardian*, September 1, www.theguardian.com/technology/2014/sep/01/how-to-attack-a-woman-who-works-in-video-games.

Fraser, N. 1990. Rethinking the public sphere: a contribution to the critique of actually existing democracy. *Social Text*, 25/26, 56–80.

Fraser, N. (2014). Transnationalizing the public sphere: on the legitimacy and efficacy of public opinion in a post-Westphalian world. In Nash, K. (ed.), *Transnationalizing the public sphere* (pp. 8–42). Cambridge, UK: Polity Press.

Fraser, N. & Honneth, A. 2003. *Redistribution or recognition? A political-philosophical exchange*, London & New York: Verso.

Freedom House (2014) Freedom in the world 2014: The annual survey of political rights and civil liberties. Lanham, MA: Rowman & Littlefield.

Freedom House (2015) Freedom in the world 2015: The annual survey of political rights and civil liberties. Lanham, MA: Rowman & Littlefield.

Fuchs, C. 2012. Social media, riots, and revolutions. *Capital & Class*, 36(3), 383–391.

Fuchs, C. 2014a. *OccupyMedia! The Occupy Movement and social media in crisis capitalism*, Winchester: Zero Books.

Fuchs, C. 2014b. *Social media: a critical introduction*, London & Thousand Oaks, CA: Sage.

Gadd, V. 2015. Twitter executive: here's how we're trying to stop abuse while preserving free speech. *Washington Post*, April 16, www.washingtonpost.com/posteverything/wp/2015/04/16/twitter-executive-heres-how-were-trying-to-stop-abuse-while-preserving-free-speech.

Gandy, I. 2014. #TwitterFail: Twitter's refusal to handle online stalkers, abusers, and haters. RH Reality Check, August 12, http://rhrealitycheck.org/article/2014/08/12/twitterfail-twitters-refusal-handle-online-stalkers-abusers-haters.

Garlick, S. 2013. Complexity, masculinity, and critical theory: revisiting Marcuse on technology, eros, and nature. *Critical Sociology*, 39(2), 223–238.

Gaudiosi, J. 2015. Mobile game revenues set to overtake console games in 2015. *Fortune*, January 15, http://fortune.com/2015/01/15/mobile-console-game-revenues-2015.

Gavey, N. 2005. *Just sex? The cultural scaffolding of rape*, New York & London: Routledge.

Gehl, R. W. 2012. Real (software) abstractions on the rise of Facebook and the fall of MySpace. *Social Text*, 30(2), 99–119.

Gerbaudo, P. 2012. *Tweets and the streets: social media and contemporary activism*, London: Pluto Press.

Gibson, W. 1984. *Neuromancer*, New York: Ace.

Gill, R. 2008. Empowerment/sexism: figuring female sexual agency in contemporary advertising. *Feminism & Psychology*, 18(1), 35–60.

Gill, R., Henwood, K. & McLean, C. 2005. Body projects and the regulation of normative masculinity. *Body & Society*, 11(1), 37–62.

Goffman, E. 1963. *Stigma: notes on the management of spoiled identity*, New York: Simon and Schuster.

Gramsci, A. 1971. *Selections from the prison notebooks of Antonio Gramsci*, New York: International Publishers.

Gray, D. & Watt, P. 2014. Giving victims a voice: joint report into sexual allegations made against Jimmy Savile. Metropolitan Police Service and the National Society for the Prevention of Cruelty to Children. www.nspcc.org.uk/globalassets/documents/research-reports/yewtree-report-giving-victims-voice-jimmy-savile.pdf

Greer, C. & McLaughlin, E. 2011. 'Trial by media': policing, the 24–7 news mediasphere and the 'politics of outrage'. *Theoretical Criminology*, 15(1), 23–46.

Greer, C. & Reiner, R. 2012. Mediated mayhem: media, crime, criminal justice. In: Maguire, M., Morgan, R. & Reiner, R. (eds.) *The Oxford handbook of criminology* (pp. 245–278). Oxford: Oxford University Press.

Habermas, J. 1984. *The theory of communicative action*, London: Heinemann Educational.

Habermas, J. 1989. *The structural transformation of the public sphere: an inquiry into a category of bourgeois society*, Cambridge: Polity Press.

Habermas, Jürgen. 2006. Political communication in media society: does democracy still enjoy an epistemic dimension? The impact of normative theory on empirical research. *Communication Theory*, 16(4), 411–426.

Hand, M. & Sandywell, B. 2002. E-topia as cosmopolis or citadel on the democratizing and de-democratizing logics of the internet, or, toward a critique of the new technological fetishism. *Theory, Culture & Society*, 19(1–2), 197–225.

Harvey, L. & Ringrose, J. 2015. Sexting, ratings and (mis) recognition: teen boys performing classed and racialized masculinities in digitally networked publics. In: Renold, E., Ringrose, J. & Egan, R. D. (eds.), *Children, sexuality and sexualization* (pp. 352–367). Basingstoke: Palgrave Macmillan.

Hayward, K. 2007. Situational crime prevention and its discontents: rational choice theory versus the 'culture of now'. *Social Policy & Administration*, 41(3), 232–250.

Hearn, A. 2010. Structuring feeling: Web 2.0, online ranking and rating, and the digital 'reputation' economy. *ephemera*, 10(3/4), 421–438.

Hearn, J. & Whitehead, A. 2006. Collateral damage: men's 'domestic' violence to women seen through men's relation with men. *Journal of Community and Criminal Justice*, 53(1), 38–56.

Herring, S. C. 1993. Gender and democracy in computer-mediated communication. *European Journal of Communication*, 3(2), 1–30.

Herring, S. C. 1999. The rhetorical dynamics of gender harassment on-line. *The Information Society*, 15(3), 151–167.

Hess, A. 2014. A former FBI agent on why it's so hard to prosecute Gamergate trolls. *Slate*, October 17, www.slate.com/blogs/xx_factor/2014/10/17/ gamergate_threats_why_it_s_so_hard_to_prosecute_the_people_targeting_zoe.html.

Hess, A. 2015a. Don't ban Yik Yak. *Slate*, October 28, http://primary.slate.com/articles/technology/users/2015/10/yik_yak_is_good_for_university_stu dents.html.

Hess, A. 2015b. How a stunt pregnancy announcement, and a miscarriage, turned Sam and Nia into YouTube stars. *Slate*, August 12, http://news.na tionalpost.com/arts/sam-and-nia-youtube-stars.

HMIC. 2013. *Mistakes were made: HMIC's review into allegations and intelligence material concerning Jimmy Savile between 1964 and 2012*. HMIC: London.

Hoffman, C. 2013. Giovanna Plowman victim of bullying after eating her own tampon. *Examiner*, January 20, www.examiner.com/article/giovanna-plowman-victim-of-bullying-after-eating-her-own-tampon.

Holland, J., Ramazanoglu, C., Sharpe, S. & Thomson, R. 1998. *The male in the head: young people, heterosexuality and power*, London: Tufnell Press.

Horkheimer, M. & Adorno, T. W. 1972. *Dialectic of enlightenment*, New York: Herder and Herder.

Howell O'Neill, P. 2014. 8chan, the central hive mind of Gamergate, is also an active pedophile network. Daily Dot, November 17, www.dailydot.com/politics/8chan-pedophiles-child-porn-gamergate/.

Huffington Post. 2013. This is how the internet is rewiring your brain, November 31, www.huffingtonpost.com.au/2013/10/30/shocking-ways-internet-rewires-brain_n_4136942.html?ir=Australia.

Human Rights Foundation. 2015. Recap: HRF puts Gabon's human rights and corruption crisis in the news, August 6, http://humanrightsfoundation.org/news/recap-hrf-puts-gabons-human-rights-and-corruption-crisis-in-the-news-00451.

Ip, C. 2014. How do we know what we know about #Gamergate? *Columbia Journalism Review*, October 23, www.cjr.org/behind_the_news/gamergate.php.

Jackson, N. 2011. As MySpace sells for $35 million, a history of the network's valuation. *The Atlantic*, June 29, www.theatlantic.com/technology/archive/2011/06/as-myspace-sells-for-35-million-a-history-of-the-networks-valuation/241224.

Jane, E. A. 2014. 'Back to the kitchen, cunt': speaking the unspeakable about online misogyny. *Continuum*, 28(4), 558–570.

Jason, Z. 2015. Game of fear: what if a stalker had an army? Zoe Quinn's ex-boyfriend was obsessed with destroying her reputation – and thousands of online strangers were eager to help. *Boston Magazine*, May, www.bostonma gazine.com/news/article/2015/04/28/gamergate.

Jenkins, H. 2006. *Convergence culture: where old and new media collide*, New York: NYU Press.

Jeong, S. 2015. *The internet of garbage*. Brighton: Forbes Media.

Jewkes, Y. 2007. 'Killed by the Internet': cyber homicides, cyber suicides and cyber sex crimes. In: Jewkes, Y. (ed.), *Crime online* (pp. 1–11). Collumpton and Portland: Willan Publishing.

Johnson, B. 2010. Privacy no longer a social norm, says Facebook founder. *The Guardian*, January 11, www.theguardian.com/technology/2010/jan/11/facebook-privacy.

Johnston, C. 2014. Chat logs show how 4chan users created #GamerGate hashtag. *Ars Technica*, September 10, http://arstechnica.com/gaming/2014/09/new-chat-logs-show-how-4chan-users-pushed-gamergate-into-the-national-spotlight.

Jones, A. 2015a. All is lost: nightmare man 'surprises' wife with her own pregnancy. *Gawker*, August 7, http://gawker.com/all-is-lost-nightmare-man-surprises-wife-with-her-ow-1722515765.

Jones, A. 2015b. Christian vlogger couple admits pregnancy was 'staged'…by God himself. *Gawker*, August 17, http://gawker.com/christian-vlogger-couple-admits-pregnancy-was-staged-1724624391.

Jones, L. M., Mitchell, K. J. & Finkelhor, D. 2013. Online harassment in context: trends from three Youth Internet Safety Surveys (2000, 2005, 2010). *Psychology of Violence*, 3(1), 53–69.

Junco, R. 2015. Yik Yak and online anonymity are good for college students. *Wired*, March 17, www.wired.com/2015/03/yik-yak-online-anonymity-good-college-students.

Karaian, L. 2015. What is self-exploitation? Rethinking the relationship between sexualization and 'sexting' in law and order times. In: Renold, E., Ringrose, J. & Egan, R. D. (eds), *Children, sexuality and sexualization* (pp. 337–351). Basingstoke: Palgrave Macmillan.

Kaufman, S. 2014. Actor Adam Baldwin: #GamerGate defeated the Left, but there will be no parade. Raw Story, November 10, www.rawstory.com/2014/11/actor-adam-baldwin-gamergate-defeated-the-left-but-there-will-be-no-parade.

Keane, J. 1995. Structural transformations of the public sphere. *Communication Review*, 1(1), 1–22.

Keen, A. 2007. *The cult of the amateur: how blogs, MySpace, YouTube, and the rest of today's user-generated media are destroying our economy, our culture, and our values*, New York: Doubleday.

Keller, J. M. 2012. Virtual feminisms. *Information, Communication & Society*, 15(3), 429–447.

Kendall, L. 2000. 'OH NO! I'M A NERD!': hegemonic masculinity on an online forum. *Gender & Society*, 14(2), 256–274.

King, J. & Cuen, L. 2015. Gamergate is a headless troll and it's bigger than ever. *Vocativ*, August 25, http://www.vocativ.com/news/224320/gamergate-leader ship-moderators.

Klettke, B., Hallford, D. J. & Mellor, D. J. 2014. Sexting prevalence and correlates: a systematic literature review. *Clinical Psychology Review*, 34(1), 44–53.

Kotzer, Z. 2014. Female game designers are being threatened with rape. Vice, January 23, www.vice.com/en_ca/read/female-game-designers-are-being-threatened-with-rape.

Kreps, D. 2015. Revenge-porn site owner Hunter Moore pleads guilty, faces prison time. *Rolling Stone*, February 20, www.rollingstone.com/culture/news/revenge-porn-site-owner-hunter-moore-pleads-guilty-faces-prison-time-20150220.

Kubas-Meyer, A. 2015. Gamergate fail: the rise of ass-kicking women in video games. *Daily Beast*, June 23, www.thedailybeast.com/articles/2015/06/23/gamergate-fail-the-rise-of-ass-kicking-women-in-video-games.html.

Lamb, M. 1998. Cybersex: Research notes on the characteristics of the visitors to online chat rooms. *Deviant Behavior*, 19(2), 121–135.

Landes, J. (ed.). 1998. *Feminism, the public and the private*. New York: Oxford University Press.

Laws, C. 2013. I've been called the 'Erin Brovkovich' of revenge porn, and for the first time ever, here is my entire uncensored story of death threats, Anonymous and the FBI. XOJane, November 21, www.xojane.com/it-happened-to-me/charlotte-laws-hunter-moore-erin-brockovich-revenge-porn.

Lawson, A. 2008. Killing children a political ritual. *The Star*, April 21, www.thestar.com/news/world/2008/04/21/killing_children_a_political_ritual.html.

Lebur, C. 2013. Gabon girl's death sparks fears of ritual killing. *Modern Ghana*, April 20, www.modernghana.com/news/459509/1/gabon-girls-death-sparks-fears-of-ritual-killings.html.

Lepoint. 2014. Au Gabon, la psychose des crimes rituels ravivée par les réseaux sociaux. *Lepoint*, April 16, www.lepoint.fr/societe/au-gabon-la-psychose-des-crimes-rituels-ravivee-par-les-reseaux-sociaux-16-04-2013-1655690_23.php.

Levy, S. 2001. *Crypto: how the code rebels beat the government – saving privacy in the digital age*, London & New York: Penguin.

Lien, T. 2013. No girls allowed: unraveling the story behind the stereotype of video games being for boys. Polygon, December 2, www.polygon.com/features/2013/12/2/5143856/no-girls-allowed.

Lindgren, S. & Linde, J. 2012. The subpolitics of online piracy: a Swedish case study. *Convergence: The International Journal of Research into New Media Technologies*, 18(2), 143–164.

Livingstone, S. 2008. Taking risky opportunities in youthful content creation: teenagers' use of social networking sites for intimacy, privacy and self-expression. *New Media & Society*, 10(3), 393–411.

Livingstone, S. 2009. *Children and the internet*, Cambridge: Polity.

Lovink, G. 2011. *Networks without a cause: a critique of social media*, Cambridge: Polity Press.

Lowenthal, L. 1961. *Literature, popular culture, and society*, Palo Alto, CA: Pacific Books.

Lumby, C. & Albury, K. 2010. Too much? Too young? The sexualisation of children debate in Australia. *Media International Australia*, 135(1), 141–152.

Lyon, D., & Bauman, Z. 2013. *Liquid surveillance: a conversation*. Cambridge & Malden, MA: Polity.

Marcuse, H. 1941. Some social implications of modern technology. *Studies in Philosophy and Social Science*, 9(1), 414–439.

Marcuse, H. 1964. *One-dimensional man: studies in the ideology of advanced industrial society*, London: Routledge.

Marwick, A. & boyd, d. 2011. To see and be seen: celebrity practice on Twitter. *Convergence: The International Journal of Research into New Media Technologies*, 17(2), 139–158.

Marwick, A. E. 2008. To catch a predator? The MySpace moral panic. *First Monday*, 13(6), http://firstmonday.org/article/view/2152/1966.

Massanari, A. 2016. #Gamergate and The Fappening: how Reddit's algorithm, governance, and culture support toxic technocultures. *New Media & Society*, forthcoming, 1–18.

Matthews, G. 1992. *The rise of public woman: women's power and woman's place in the United States 1630–1970*, New York: Oxford University Press.

McCarthy, C. 2009. Twitter co-founder: we'll have made it when you shut up about us. *CNet*, June 3, www.cnet.com/news/twitter-co-founder-well-have-made-it-when-you-shut-up-about-us.

McGuire, M. 2007. *Hypercrime: the new geometry of harm*, Oxon and New York: Routledge-Cavendish.

McKee, A. 2004. *The public sphere: an introduction*, Cambridge: Cambridge University Press.

McMillan, R. 2013. The Friendster autopsy: how a social network dies. *Wired*, February 27, www.wired.com/2013/02/friendster-autopsy.

McNally, V. 2014. Zoe Quinn released 4chan #Gamergate chat logs, further tarnishing the movement's reputation. The Mary Sue, September 8, www.themarysue.com/gamergate-chat-logs.

McNeal, S. & Zarrell, R. 2015. Doctors cast doubt on viral video stars Sam and Nia's pregnancy claims. Buzzfeed, August 17, www.buzzfeed.com/stephaniemcneal/people-are-doubting-vloggers-sam-nias-viral-pregnancy-announ–.dwK47NmaB.

McRobbie, A. 2004. Notes on postfeminism and popular culture: Bridget Jones and the new gender regime. In: Harris, A. (ed.), *All about the girl: culture, power and identity* (pp. 3–14). New York and London: Routledge.

McRobbie, A. 2008. *The aftermath of feminism: gender, culture and social change*, London: Sage.

Merlan, A. 2015. Rep. Katherine Clark: the FBI needs to make Gamergate 'a priority'. Jezebel, March 10, http://jezebel.com/rep-katherine-clark-the-fbi-needs-to-make-gamergate-a-1690599361.

Middleton, W. 2015. Tipping points and the accommodation of the abuser: the case of ongoing incestuous abuse during adulthood. *International Journal of Crime, Justice and Social Democracy*, 4(2), 4–17.

Mitchell, K. J., Finkelhor, D., Jones, L. M. & Wolak, J. 2010. Use of Social Networking Sites in Online Sex Crimes Against Minors: an examination of national incidence and means of utilization. *Journal of Adolescent Health*, 47(2), 183–190.

Mitchell, K. J., Finkelhor, D. & Wolak, J. 2001. Risk factors for and impact of online sexual solicitation of youth. *Jama*, 285(23), 3011–3014.

Mitchell, K. J., Jones, L. M., Finkelhor, D. & Wolak, J. 2013. Understanding the decline in unwanted online sexual solicitations for U.S. youth 2000–2010: findings from three Youth Internet Safety Surveys. *Child Abuse & Neglect*, 37(12), 1225–1236.

Moore, T. 2013. In defense of the attention whore. Jezebel, May 23, http://jezebel.com/in-defense-of-the-attention-whore-509362561.

Morahan-Martin, J. 1998. The gender gap in internet use: why men use the internet more than women – a literature review. *CyberPsychology & Behavior*, 1(1), 3–10.

Moreno, M. A., Parks, M. R., Zimmerman, F. J., Brito, T. E. & Christakis, D. A. 2009. Display of health risk behaviors on myspace by adolescents: prevalence and associations. *Archives of Pediatrics & Adolescent Medicine*, 163(1), 27–34.

Morrison, K. 2015. Snapchat is the fastest growing social network, *Adweek*, July 28, www.adweek.com/socialtimes/snapchat-is-the-fastest-growing-social-network-infographic/624116.

Mulvey, L. 1999. Visual pleasure and narrative cinema. In: Braudy, L. & Cohen, M. (eds.), *Film theory and criticism: introductory readings* (pp. 833–844). New York: Oxford University Press.

Nakamura, L. 2014. Gender and race online. In: Graham, M. & Dutton, W. (eds), *Society and the internet: how networks of information and communication are changing our lives* (pp. 81–98). Oxford: Oxford University Press.

news.com.au. 2015. Intimate photos of around 400 Adelaide women have been posted on a US site in revenge porn. June 18, www.news.com.au/technology/online/intimate-photos-of-around-400-adelaide-women-have-been-posted-on-a-us-site-in-revenge-porn/story-fnjwmwrh-1227403257763.

Norris, P. 2001. *Digital divide: civic engagement, information poverty and the internet worldwide*, Cambridge: Cambridge University Press.

O'Reilly, T. 2005. What is Web 2.0: design patterns and business models for the next generation of software. www.oreilly.com/pub/a/web2/archive/what-is-web-20.html?page=1.

Pachal, P. 2011. Why Friendster died: social media isn't a game. *PC Mag*, April 29, http://au.pcmag.com/web-sites-products/10248/opinion/why-friendster-died-social-media-isnt-a-game.

Pariser, E. 2011. *The filter bubble: what the internet is hiding from you*, London & New York: Penguin.

Parkin, S. 2014. Zoe Quinn's depression quest. *New Yorker*, September 9, www.newyorker.com/tech/elements/zoe-quinns-depression-quest.

Patterson, M. & Elliott, R. 2002. Negotiating masculinities: advertising and the inversion of the male gaze. *Consumption Markets & Culture*, 5(3), 231–249.

Pew Research Centre. 2014. Online harrasment. www.pewinternet.org/2014/10/22/online-harassment..

Phillips, W. 2015. *This is why we can't have nice things: mapping the relationship between online trolling and mainstream culture*, Cambridge, MA & London: MIT Press.

Pless, M. 2015. Actually, it's about ethics in Stockholm Syndrome. Idle Dilletannte, October 31, http://idledillettante.com/2015/10/31/actually-its-about-ethics-in-stockholm-syndrome.

Poster, M. 1997. CyberDemocracy: internet and the public sphere. In: Porter, D. (ed.), *Internet culture* (pp. 201–218). New York & London: Routledge.

Proctor, S., Galloway, R., Chaloner, R., Jones, C., & Thompson, D. 2014. *The report of the investigation into matters relating to Savile at Leeds Teaching Hospitals NHS Trust*. Leeds: Leeds Teaching Hopsitals NHS Trust.

Renold, E. & Ringrose, J. 2011. Schizoid subjectivities?: Re-theorizing teen girls' sexual cultures in an era of 'sexualization'. *Journal of Sociology*, 47(4), 389–409.

Reporters Without Borders. 2012. Journalists harassed for violating taboo on ritual killings. *Reporters Without Borders*, October 24, http://en.rsf.org/gabon-journalists-harassed-for-violating-24-10-2012,43576.html.

Reuters. 2013. YouTube stats: site has 1 billion active users each month. *Huffington Post*, March 20, www.huffingtonpost.com/2013/03/21/youtube-stats_n_2922543.html.

Ringrose, J. 2013. *Postfeminist Education? Girls and the sexual politics of schooling*, London and New York: Routledge.

Ringrose, J., Harvey, L., Gill, R. & Livingstone, S. 2013. Teen girls, sexual double standards and 'sexting': gendered value in digital image exchange. *Feminist Theory*, 14(3), 305–323.

Ritzer, G. & Jurgenson, N. 2010. Production, consumption, prosumption: the nature of capitalism in the age of the digital 'prosumer'. *Journal of Consumer Culture*, 10(1), 13–36.

Rivlin, G. (2006) Wallflower at the web party. New York Times, October 15: http://www.nytimes.com/2006/10/15/business/yourmoney/15friend.html?_r=2.

Robinson, M. 2014. Revealed: the glass eye Jimmy Savile stole from a corpse and made into a necklace that he wore on final Top of the Pops – where he also groped a child. *Daily Mail*, June 28, www.dailymail.co.uk/news/article-2672395/Glass-eye-stolen-corpse-Savile-necklace-sold-charity-auction-75-wore-final-Top-Pops-groped-child.html.

Roesner, F., Safavi-Naini, R. & Kohno, T. 2014. Sex, lies, or kittens? Investigating the use of snapchat's self-destructing messages. In: Cristin, N. S.-N. R. (eds), *Financial Cryptography and Data Security: 18th International Conference, FC 2014, Christ Church, Barbados, March 3–7, 2014 Revised Selected Papers* (pp. 64–76). New York and London: Springer.

Romano, A. 2014. 4chan hacks and doxes Zoe Quinn's biggest supporter. Daily Dot, August 22, www.dailydot.com/geek/4chan-hacks-phil-fish-over-his-defense-of-zoe-quinn.

Salter, M. 2008. Out of the shadows: re-envisioning the debate on ritual abuse. In: Perskin, P. & Noblitt, R. (eds) *Ritual abuse in the twenty-first century: Psychological, forensic, social and political considerations* (pp. 153–174). Brandon, OR: Robert D. Reed publishing.

Salter, M. 2012. Invalidation: a neglected dimensions of gender-based violence and inequality. *International Journal for Crime and Justice*, 1(1), 3–13.

Salter, M. 2013a. Justice and revenge in online counter-publics: emerging responses to sexual violence in the age of social media. *Crime, Media, Culture*, 9(3), 225–242.

Salter, M. 2013b. *Organised sexual abuse*, London: Glasshouse/Routledge.

Salter, M. 2016. Privates in the online public: sex(ting) and reputation on social media. *New Media & Society*, forthcoming.

Salter, M. & Crofts, T. 2015. Responding to revenge porn: challenges to online legal impunity. In: Comella, L. & Tarrant, L. (eds.) *New views on pornography: sexuality, politics and the law* (pp. 233–256). Santa Barbara, CA: Praeger.

Salter, M., Crofts, T. & Lee, M. 2013. Beyond criminalisation and responsibilisation: sexting, gender and young people. *Current Issues in Criminal Justice*, 24(3), 301–316.

Schneider, S. M. 1996. Creating a democratic public sphere through political discussion: a case study of abortion conversation on the internet. *Social Science Computer Review*, 14(4), 373–393.

Senft, T. M. 2008. *Camgirls: celebrity and community in the age of social networks*, New York: Peter Lang.

Shaw, A. 2012. Do you identify as a gamer? Gender, race, sexuality, and gamer identity. *New Media & Society*, 14(1), 28–44.

Shirky, C. 2008. *Here comes everybody: the power of organizing without organizations*, London, Penguin.

Siklos, R. 2005. News Corp. to acquire owner of Myspace.com. *New York Times*, July 18, www.nytimes.com/2005/07/18/business/18cnd-newscorp.html?_r=0.

Sinders, C. 2015. That time the internet sent a SWAT team to my mom's house. Boing Boing, July 24, https://boingboing.net/2015/07/24/that-time-the-internet-sent-a.html.

Sontag, S. 1977. *On photography*, London: Penguin.

Southworth, C., Finn, J., Dawson, S., Fraser, C. & Tucker, S. 2007. Intimate partner violence, technology, and stalking. *Violence Against Women*, 13(8), 842–856.

Spender, D. 1996. *Nattering on the net: women, power and cyberspace*, Melbourne: Spinifex Press.

Styles, A. 2012. Rainbow milk spin on fully sick music video. *WA Today*, March 22, www.watoday.com.au/wa-news/rainbow-milk-spin-on-fully-sick-music-video-20120321-1vk4q.html.

Summers, A. 1975. *Damned whores and God's police*, Melbourne: Allen Lane.

Sussman, N. M. & Tyson, D. H. 2000. Sex and power: gender differences in computer-mediated interactions. *Computers in Human Behavior*, 16(4), 381–394.

Tapscott, D. & Williams, A. D. 2008. *Wikinomics: how mass collaboration changes everything*, New York: Penguin.

Tiku, N. & Newton, C. 2015. Twitter CEO: 'we suck at dealing with abuse'. *The Verge*, February 4, www.theverge.com/2015/2/4/7982099/twitter-ceo-sent-memo-taking-personal-responsibility-for-the.

Tolman, D. L. 2002. *Dilemmas of desire: teenage girls talk about sexuality*, Cambridge, MA & London, Harvard University Press.

Turner, F. 2010. *From counterculture to cyberculture: Stewart Brand, the Whole Earth Network, and the rise of digital utopianism*, Chicago: University of Chicago Press.

UN Women. 2015. Cyber violence against women and girls: a world-wide wake up call. www.unwomen.org/~/media/headquarters/attachments/sections/library/publications/2015/cyber_violence_genderreport.pdf?v=1&d=20150924T154259.

Valentine, G. 1989. The geography of women's fear. *Area*, 21(4), 385–390.

Van Dijck, J. 2013. *The culture of connectivity: a critical history of social media*, Oxford: Oxford University Press.

van Zoonen, L. 2002. Gendering the internet. *European Journal of Communication*, 17(1), 5–23.

Vandello, J. A. & Cohen, D. 2003. Male honor and female fidelity: implicit cultural scripts that perpetuate domestic violence. *Journal of Personality and Social Psychology*, 84(5), 997.

Wall, D. 2001. Cybercrimes and the internet. In: Wall, D. (ed.) *Crime and the internet* (pp. 1–17). Oxon and New York: Routledge.

Warner, M. 2002. *Publics and counterpublics*. New York: Zone Books.

Weintraub, J. 1997. The theory and politics of the public/private distinction. In: Weintraub, J. & Kumar, K. (eds), *Public and private in thought and practice: perspectives on a grand dichotomy* (Vol. 1, pp. 1–42). Chicago, IL & London: University of Chicago Press.

West, L. 2014. Twitter doesn't think these rape and death threats are harassment. Daily Dot, December 23, www.dailydot.com/opinion/twitter-harassment-rape-death-threat-report.

Williams, A. A. & Marquez, B. A. 2015. The lonely Selfie King: selfies and the conspicuous prosumption of gender and race. *International Journal of Communication*, 9, 13, 1775–1787.

Winlow, S., Hall, S., Treadwell, J. & Briggs, D. 2015. *Riots and political protest: notes from the post-political present*, New York & London: Routledge.

Wintour, P. 2009. Facebook and Bebo risk 'infantalising' the human mind. *Guardian*, February 24, www.theguardian.com/uk/2009/feb/24/social-networking-site-changing-childrens-brains.

Wolf, A. 2015. Why women shouldn't have to form girl-gangs to deal with dickheads on the internet. Medium, December 4, https://medium.com/@Asher_Wolf/why-women-shouldn-t-have-to-form-girl-gangs-to-deal-with-dickheads-on-the-internet-613e8626de64#.d7sv5fxeo.

Wright, J. 2015. 'Enough is enough': Clementine Ford to lodge police complaint over trolling. *Sydney Morning Herald*, June 26, www.smh.com.au/national/enough-is-enough-clementine-ford-to-lodge-police-complaint-over-trolling-20150626-ghyr8w.html.

Yar, M. 2014. *The cultural imaginary of the Internet: virtual utopias and dystopias*, Basingstoke & New York: Palgrave Macmillan.

Yiannopoloulos, M. 2014. Feminist bullies tearing the video game industry apart. Brietbart, September 1, www.breitbart.com/london/2014/09/01/lying-greedy-promiscuous-feminist-bullies-are-tearing-the-video-game-industry-apart.

INDEX

Page numbers in **bold** refer to figures.